Jake's Women

JAKE'S
WOMEN

BY
Neil Simon

RANDOM HOUSE NEW YORK

FOR MY LOVING DAUGHTER BRYN

JAKE'S WOMEN, by Neil Simon, produced by Emanuel Azenberg, opened in New York City on March 24, 1992, following a pre-Broadway engagement at the Stevens Center for the Performing Arts in Winston-Salem, North Carolina, with the following cast:

JAKE	Alan Alda
MAGGIE	Helen Shaver
KAREN	Brenda Vaccaro
MOLLY (AT 12)	Genia Michaela
MOLLY (AT 21)	Tracy Pollan
EDITH	Joyce Van Patten
JULIE	Kate Burton
SHEILA	Talia Balsam

Gene Saks was the director. The scenery and costumes were designed by Santo Loquasto, the lighting by Tharon Musser, the sound by Tom Morse, and Peter Lawrence was the production supervisor.

Act One

The action of the play takes place both in JAKE's apartment and in his mind. The apartment is minimal, his mind is overflowing. There are no walls, no windows, no sense of place, and even time is indefinite.

There is, however, a staircase that goes up at an angle and stops at a second level. This is JAKE's office. A desk, a chair and a word processor. Nothing else. Next to it, a single door.

Downstairs is a sofa and a few chairs.

The people in JAKE's imagination hopefully or seemingly appear from nowhere and leave the same way. Lights should help achieve this. It's important that they can appear and leave almost instantly.

As the curtain rises, JAKE, a man in his early fifties, is upstairs at work at his processor. He types, leans back to think, types again. The phone rings. He stays lost in thought. It rings twice more before he picks it up, irritated by the interruption.

JAKE *(Into the phone)* Hello? . . . Yes, Karen, I'm working . . . No, I'm not *always* working, I'm just working now . . . Okay, so I'm working every time you call, what is it, Karen? . . . No, Maggie isn't home yet. *(Losing patience)* We're all having dinner Saturday night, yes, I know.

> *(MAGGIE, an attractive woman in her late thirties, appears downstairs, unnoticed by JAKE. She stands and thumbs through a magazine)*

JAKE *(Into the phone)* Primolo's restaurant on Sixty-third, I know . . . Karen, why do you always have to confirm what we've already confirmed? . . . I don't talk to you like a stranger, I talk to you like my sister . . . You don't feel I do? . . . Do you want me to confirm

3

that you're my sister? . . . Karen, I have to get back to work . . . I don't know what I'm writing, I haven't read it yet . . . I'm hanging up now, Karen. Please don't call back to confirm I've hung up on you. Goodbye . . .

(He hangs up)

MAGGIE *(Looking through a magazine)* You are, you know.

JAKE I am what?

MAGGIE Always working.

JAKE I stop when you come home, don't I?

MAGGIE You stop typing but your mind keeps working.

JAKE Not out of choice. My mind has a mind of its own . . . Why did I send for you?

MAGGIE Beats me. I'm still out there on Forty-eighth Street looking for a cab. You see what I mean? I'm just a thought in your head right now and you're so busy working, you can't even think of why you just thought of me.

JAKE No, no. I remember. I was just thinking about the first day we met.

MAGGIE You love to play back that tape, don't you?

JAKE Do it with me, Maggie. The way we met.

MAGGIE You do it too much, Jake.

JAKE I must need it. Come on, Maggie, do it.

MAGGIE *(She looks at her watch)* Well, I've got ten minutes before I get home. Why not? Okay . . . *(She pre-
tends to pick up a glass. They stand on opposite sides of the
stage)* East Hampton. Eight years ago. The July Fourth
party at the Tabacks' . . . A sunset.

JAKE A beautiful sunset.

MAGGIE A beautiful sunset. I'm wearing a light blue
Laura Ashley dress that I borrowed from my friend,
Laura Ashley, who unfortunately is *not* the designer,
so it hangs a little . . . I'm on my second Margarita,
feeling a little nervous because this is the In crowd and
I'm an Out girl and don't know a soul here, including
the guy who brought me . . . Then I notice you notic-
ing me so I pretend not to notice because you look kind
of sexy and intelligent and I don't think I can handle
sexy and intelligent on two Margaritas on an empty
stomach.

JAKE Will you just skip to the part when we meet?

MAGGIE Hey, Jake. These words are coming out of your
mind. You're the one who just made yourself sexy and
intelligent.

JAKE Okay okay okay . . . So I notice you and you notice
me. Then you turn to talk to this Yuppie couple.

5

MAGGIE   So I turn to talk to this Yuppie couple, both dressed in white slacks, white blazers and white buckskins, looking like two bandaged index fingers. *(To the imaginary couple, she laughs heartily)* Oh, God, I haven't made up my mind *who* to vote for ... No, I understand the issues, I just don't know who's running.

JAKE   *(To an imaginary friend)*   Frank! Hey, Frank. Who's the girl in the light blue dress? ... *That's* Laura Ashley? ... No, not the dress. The girl. Well, ask because I'd like to know.

MAGGIE   *(To the couple)*   It's Maggie ... No, I don't think we have ... Oh, my God. You're *that* Ralph Lauren ... How nice. I thought you two were always on safari.

(She drinks)

JAKE   *(Pushing through the crowd)*   Pardon me. Coming through ... Oh, hi, Barbara ... You *did* like the book? Oh, I'm so glad ... The *L.A. Times?* No, I didn't read it ... You *mailed* me a bad review? How thoughtful ... Excuse me.

MAGGIE   *(To a man)*   Oh, hello. Nice to meet you, Ed. *(She shakes his hand)* You look so familiar. Are you an actor? ... What do you mean, sort of? ... Oh, God. You're Mayor Koch, aren't you?

JAKE   Excuse me. Coming through ... Oh, hi, Martha ... Of course I'll give. What's the charity? ... The Homeless of East Hampton? ... You mean the ones who couldn't rent a house this summer?

MAGGIE   Would you excuse me, Mr. Ed? Mr. Koch . . . I see someone who knows where the bathroom is.

(*MAGGIE and JAKE turn and bump into each other. She spills her drink*)

MAGGIE   Oh, God, I am *so* sorry.

JAKE *(He looks at his crotch)*   That's okay . . .

MAGGIE   Would you like my napkin?

JAKE *(He looks at his crotch again)*   Well, it's an awkward place to be rubbing.

MAGGIE   Well, *I* wasn't going to rub it. I thought *you* would.

JAKE   It'll dry. No one will notice if you stand in front of me for a while.

MAGGIE   Well, I'm not feeling all that well. There's Mayor Koch. He might want to stand in front of you.

(*She starts to go; he blocks her*)

JAKE   Are you—here with anyone?

MAGGIE   Yes, I'm with a date . . . Charley something.

JAKE   That's odd. My date is Sybil something.

MAGGIE   Oh? Maybe they're married.

JAKE   Gee, I hope so . . . Are you here for the summer?

MAGGIE   Nooo . . . Are you?

JAKE   Nooo . . . Amazing how many things we have in common . . . Is your name Jake?

MAGGIE   No. It's Maggie. Do I look like a Jake?

JAKE   No. I do. I'm just looking for a hook in this conversation . . . Could I er . . . buy you dinner?

MAGGIE   Oh, that's very nice of you but I think the food here is free . . . Well, it was nice meeting you, Jake.

JAKE   This can't be goodbye.

MAGGIE   It won't be. We'll meet again.

JAKE   When?

MAGGIE   (*She looks at her watch*)   Well, I'll be home for dinner in ten minutes. Go back to work, Jake. Living out the past is not going to get us through the future.

(*She puts down the glass and starts out*)

JAKE   Damnit, Maggie! Can't we just have ten good minutes together? Because I'm afraid tonight may not be so wonderful.

MAGGIE   Really? Well, I don't know what's going to happen tonight, Jake, do I? And that scares you. Because you can never control what I say when reality begins.

(She leaves. JAKE faces the audience)

JAKE *(To the audience)*   She's right, you know. Reality is
a bummer. God, how much better writing is. *(He points
to his office)* That little room up there is eight by ten feet
but to me it's the world. The universe! You don't get
to play God, you get to *be* God! . . . Push time back-
wards or forwards or put it on hold. Bend it, twist it,
tie it in knots or tie it in ribbons, the choice is yours.
And oh, what choices . . . The downside? You get to
be a slave to the thing you love. Eight hours go by up
there in ten minutes and that ten minutes is captured
forever on paper . . . but the eight hours of your life is
gone and you'll never see those again, brother . . . How
much living have I missed these last thirty years?
. . . And is creative pleasure better than real pleasure?
. . . We're all writers in a sense, aren't we? . . . You're
driving in your car to work, having an imaginary conversation with your wife. She says this, you say that,
she says that, you say this. She's so damn stubborn and
intractible—only she's not saying it. You wrote it!
You're bright, witty and clever and she's a pain in the
ass. You win the argument and she's not even there,
what the hell kind of victory is that? *(He looks at his
watch)* Maggie'll be home soon, knowing something is
up with us and she'll be armed to the teeth with
honesty. Honesty can bring a writer to his knees and
Maggie's got enough to bring me to my hips. *(He calls
out)* Karen! I need help. *(To the audience)* My sister
Karen is no wizard but she *is* family. Married, divorced, went to NYU Film School. Made a three-hour
student film of *her,* just sitting on a kitchen chair, called
Loneliness . . . But she'll be on my side. Loving, encour-
aging, sympathetic, because that's how I need her and

that's how I'll make her. And no matter what she's doing, she'll come the minute I think of her. *(He calls out)* Karen! It's Jake.

> *(KAREN comes out. She's about forty, dressed in a rather unflattering dress)*

KAREN   What? I'm here. Stop yelling. You have to think of me now? I was watching *The Godfather I, II* and *III* . . . If he makes four, five and six, forget it, I need a life . . . What's wrong, Jake?

JAKE   It's Maggie and me. We're having trouble and I need advice, Karen.

KAREN   Is she here? Do you want me to speak to her? Where is she, I'll talk to her.

JAKE   If she were here, how could you talk to her, Karen? *(He points to his head)* You're here, here in my head.

KAREN   I never know how that works. When I'm here, I can talk to you. But when someone *else* is here, I can't talk to *them*. It's very confusing Jake. I feel like I'm in a Woody Allen movie.

JAKE *(He turns to the audience)*   The interesting dilemma here is not "Why is Karen irritating me now," but why am I making her irritate me?

KAREN   I'm irritating you now, aren't I?

JAKE   A little. It's nothing. It's a mind exercise. I keep

writing in my head like magicians twirl a coin over
their fingers.

KAREN   Don't write me, Jake. Let me be me. You have
such a distorted picture of me these days.

JAKE   *I* do?

KAREN   Where did you find this dress I'm wearing? This
dress is not me. Bette Midler does a concert in a dress
like this.

JAKE   I'm sorry. I was working. I didn't have time to go
shopping for clothes, Karen . . . I wanted to talk to you
now. I need advice and you're the only one in the
world who can help me now . . . Would you?

KAREN   Of course. I *want* to hear. I care about you. I
worry about you. You're my brother, I love you . . .
See, that's a good speech. That's how I should talk.
Giving, caring, nurturing. Make a note of that.

JAKE   *(To the audience)*   They make you pay for these
conversations. I used to think of my mother and she'd
make me eat a whole imaginary dinner while I talked.

KAREN   So what is it, Jake? Tell me what's wrong.

JAKE   I think Maggie's getting ready to leave me.

KAREN   Don't tell me. Oh, my God, no. Why? What
happened?

JAKE   A lot of things that never should have happened.

KAREN Alright, don't jump to conclusions . . . Don't try to guess what's going on in someone else's mind. I used to worry that Harry was going to leave me too.

JAKE But he *did* leave you.

KAREN Because I kept saying, "You're going to leave me one day, I know it." It drove him crazy . . . Besides, we had big problems. You and Maggie had eight good years together. She loves you, that I would bet my life on.

JAKE She's been seeing another man.

KAREN I'm such a bad judge of character. Are you positive, Jake?

JAKE It's someone new in her office. I don't know if he means something to her or if it's just a symptom of what's wrong with us.

KAREN What *is* wrong with you?

JAKE Something stopped.

KAREN I am so depressed. Is there something wrong with our family, Jake? Mom got divorced. Pop got divorced. I got divorced. Now you're getting divorced.

JAKE Mom and Pop is one divorce. And I'm not divorced yet. Don't make it an epidemic, Karen.

KAREN Have you been seeing anyone?

JAKE   Me? No.

KAREN   You haven't been seeing another woman?

JAKE   Didn't I just say no?

KAREN   Who's the other woman?

JAKE   An actress, about a year ago. It only lasted about three weeks.

KAREN   You mean if it's under a month, it's not an affair? Every man in America is looking for a calendar like that.

JAKE   I expected you to be supportive.

KAREN   No, you expected me to say what you want to hear. Alright, how's this? . . . "You're entitled to an affair, Jake. You work hard. It would kill Momma to hear but she's dead anyway so what do *you* care?"

JAKE   Karen, I don't need you to make me feel guilty.

KAREN   Yes, you do. I don't mind. I'm not working anyway . . . So tell me, are you still seeing this tramp?

JAKE   She's not a tramp . . . No. It's over. The truth is, I love Maggie more now than I ever have in my life. I don't want to lose her, Karen. If I lose her, I lose everything.

KAREN   Oh, Jake, Jake. You're so dependent on women. I've always known that. I wish I could hold you right now. I want to grab you in my arms the way Momma did and make you feel wonderful and safe and loved. I'm sorry Julie died. I'm sorry Maggie is so unhappy. But you have me, Jake. You can count on me . . . This is another good speech. Give me more lines like this. This is a woman you could like.

JAKE   Everyone likes you, Karen.

KAREN   So why can't I make a marriage work? Don't end up alone like me, Jake. I live in the movies, night after night, and you can't be happy living in a popcorn world . . . No! See that's crappy dialogue. You're getting even with me now for that crack about Momma.

JAKE   I'm sorry. I'll fax you the rewrites tomorrow, okay?

KAREN   Does that mean I'm going?

JAKE   *(He turns his head)*   No. I hear Maggie coming up the stairs. Stay a few minutes.

KAREN   I'm in your head. How am I going to get out, when you sneeze?

JAKE   *(To the audience)*   Maggie'll come in with a big smile on her face, always hiding her true feelings . . . "Hi, hon. Sorry I'm late."

(*MAGGIE comes in carrying her leather case*)

MAGGIE   Hi, hon. I actually found a taxi.

JAKE *(To the audience)* Close enough.

MAGGIE Do you mind if we call in for Chinese? I'm too tired to eat low-fat food tonight.

KAREN She gets to dress so pretty and I have to wear this ugly shmata.

MAGGIE *(She goes to Jake and kisses his cheek)* Ohh, you smell good. You took a shower. That's what I need. You get so grimy from ambition.

(She starts upstairs)

JAKE You going to be long?

MAGGIE Not if I use soap. Why?

JAKE I just thought we'd talk.

MAGGIE Before dinner?

JAKE *(He shrugs)* Before. During. After.

MAGGIE Really? It's been years since we had a marathon conversation . . . Sure. Just let me wash my face, I'll be right down . . . Anything I should feel nervous about?

JAKE Depends on what makes you nervous.

MAGGIE . . . Answers like that.

(She is gone)

KAREN   Oh, Jake, Jake! You're asking for trouble.

JAKE   What do you want me to do, forget about this other guy?

KAREN   No. Just wait. Bring it up on your fiftieth anniversary.

JAKE   I really love you, Karen. I make you sound silly and foolish and irritating. The clown with a heart of gold. You'll meet the right man. Trust me. I'll look myself.

KAREN   Find him, don't think of him. I don't want a man who dresses worse than me.

(*She is gone. MAGGIE appears upstairs, with a towel draped around her neck*)

JAKE (*Quietly*)   Round one!

MAGGIE (*She makes a drink*)   So what kind of day did you have . . . she asks cautiously.

JAKE   I worked. I spoke to Karen.

MAGGIE   Oh. How is she?

JAKE   Lonely, miserable, frustrated. Not bad, actually . . . She's having a dinner party this Saturday. We're invited. We have to find her a date, which is why she's having the party.

MAGGIE   *This* Saturday?

JAKE   Yes.

MAGGIE   I have to go to Philadelphia on Saturday. I told you that.

JAKE   No. You said you *thought* you had to go.

MAGGIE   Yes. I said, "I think I have to go to Philadelphia on Saturday."

JAKE   "I think I'm going" is indefinite. "I'm going" is "I'll be back on Sunday." Or do you *think* you'll be back on Sunday?

MAGGIE   I will be back on Sunday. Are you in a lousy mood or do I just *think* you are?

JAKE   Sort of a lousy mood.

MAGGIE   Yes, I sort of noticed . . . This isn't what you wanted to talk about, is it, Jake?

JAKE   No.

MAGGIE   Something else then.

JAKE   Yes.

MAGGIE *(She smiles)*   Okay. What?

JAKE   I'm thinking.

MAGGIE *(Lightly)*   You looking for a topic?

JAKE No. I have a topic.

MAGGIE What is it, Jake? You look so pained. *(He doesn't answer)* Tell me. I'm not going anywhere.

JAKE I want to get the first sentence right. It's important.

MAGGIE The first sentence is?

JAKE It's the writer in me. Always afraid I'll lose my audience. Did you ever read *The Naked and the Dead*? . . . Great first sentence.

MAGGIE What was it?

JAKE "Nobody could sleep."

MAGGIE Yeah. Great first sentence alright . . . What's yours, Jake?

JAKE *(He pauses)* . . . Do you want out of this marriage?

MAGGIE *(She looks at him, stunned, then lets out a breath of her own)* Well, you've just topped Norman Mailer . . . Is this what this conversation is going to be about?

JAKE Well, let's see if it turns into a conversation first.

MAGGIE Where did this come from, Jake? And why now? Isn't this the kind of talk one prepares for? Take the phone off the hook, get out a bottle of scotch?

JAKE You get the phone, I'll get the scotch.

MAGGIE   I thought the reason you were in a lousy mood was because I couldn't have dinner with Karen on Saturday. Shows you where my mind must be.

JAKE   I don't *know* where, Maggie. Tell me.

MAGGIE   Whoa, Jake. I gave you time to think of your first sentence. Give me a chance to get my second wind . . . Why not yesterday, Jake? Or last week or last month? Did something happen today that never happened before?

JAKE   Yes.

MAGGIE   What?

JAKE   I decided to ask you.

MAGGIE   I see. Well, I guess sleeping back to back for the last few weeks doesn't make this *too* much of a surprise . . . Okay. You want to know if I want out of this marriage? The answer is "No, I do not want out of this marriage."

JAKE   I'm glad to hear it. So everything is fine.

MAGGIE   I didn't say it was.

JAKE   I didn't think it was.

MAGGIE   No, everything is *not* fine, Jake. Does that come as a shock to you?

JAKE   No. It's been obvious for months. So why haven't either of us talked about it before?

MAGGIE   We talk about it every day. In the lack of warmth we show each other. The way you sometimes don't even acknowledge me when I walk in the door.

JAKE   On the nights I'm lucky enough to still be up when you walk in.

MAGGIE   Yes, I've been working a lot more than I used to. Moving up the corporate ladder has its drawbacks, I'm sorry. Are we just going to stand here matching complaints? Where are we going with this?

JAKE   I don't know. It's our first trip . . . Are we in trouble, Maggie, or are we in *big* trouble?

MAGGIE   I love how *I* get to be the one on the witness stand. I don't know, Jake. We're in trouble. That's more than we've ever been before so the size of it seems irrelevant.

JAKE   Really? I'd hate to get a report like that from my radiologist. "Well, there's something there, Jake, but the size of it is irrelevant."

MAGGIE   Jesus, I love what you consider a "talk before dinner" . . . What have you got in mind for "during and after"?

JAKE   It's amazing but I don't even know what you're feeling right now. Are you hurt? Are you frightened? Angry? Defensive? What?

MAGGIE *(She snaps it out)* *Claustrophobic!* Isolated! Airless! Atrophying! . . . Christ, I can't believe I'm saying these things. This is dangerous, Jake. Let's put it off for a while. Please! Maybe it'll even go away in the morning.

JAKE Go away? After "Claustrophobic? Airless? Atrophying?" . . . Those words have a certain permanency. They tend to stick to your ribs.

MAGGIE Christ, you wanted this conversation, Jake. Not me. Isolated and airless are painful things to say and I'm sure to hear, but probably a lot less terrifying than the death of a marriage . . . but I guess we'd better get on with it . . . Okay. I have a first sentence for you, Jake . . . How about separating for six months just to give us some breathing space?

JAKE *(Stunned)* Separate for six months? . . . That's a lot of breathing space. That's about as big as Arizona . . . How long have you been thinking about this?

MAGGIE It just came up. More or less impromptu.

JAKE Do you actually think after six months apart, we'd be able to get together again?

MAGGIE Why not?

JAKE Why not? Half our problems are based on the fact that we're apart three or four months of the year to begin with. I don't understand how separating is the answer to being separated too much.

MAGGIE   I need the time, Jake.

JAKE   For what?

MAGGIE   For myself. I feel lost, out of control. I feel like I'm skiing down a mountain without a pole and there's nothing but trees and rocks at the bottom.

JAKE   Maybe I could be there to catch you.

MAGGIE   Catch me? I thought you were the one who pushed me . . . I didn't mean that. Oh, God, I'm so lousy at being unhappy.

JAKE   Don't you want this marriage?

MAGGIE   I have always wanted this marriage. I would give anything to go back and start it over from the beginning. But you only get one beginning to a marriage.

JAKE   Who says? Why can't we go back? Why don't we get married again. *(She dismisses it)* I'm serious. New wedding ring. New party. Different hors d'oeuvres. They're probably cold by now . . . It's possible if you want it badly enough.

MAGGIE   Thank you, Jake. That's a very sweet offer.

JAKE   Then take it.

MAGGIE   We're having enough trouble making this marriage work, let alone starting a new one.

JAKE   I don't think we should separate. I think it would be the end of us.

MAGGIE   Jake, don't you see me? Don't you see how much I've changed? I can't stop running. I run for taxis, for planes, for elevators. I run for analyst sessions and lunch appointments. I run ten miles every week-end and it's still not far enough or fast enough. I'm no good for anybody until I learn to stop running and find out what it is I'm running from. And if I'm still run-ning six months from now, there won't be anything left of me worth being married to.

JAKE   I love you, Maggie.

MAGGIE   I love you too, Jake. At least we have that to hang on to. That's worth waiting six months for, isn't it?

JAKE   It's also worth staying here and fighting for.

MAGGIE   NO! I don't *want* to fight for it. I've tried so hard this last year to *talk* to you but I always ended up just listening. We started off with a marriage and ended up with a monologue. You never listen, Jake. Not even to what I'm trying to say now. You just want it to be better without even wanting to know what's wrong. We shouldn't be fighting for our marriage, we should have been living it.

JAKE   Then let's start tonight because six months apart will kill us.

MAGGIE   So will forcing me to stay. I'm sorry, Jake.

Maybe there is a chance for us, but not with a quick resolution. I have to get in a hot tub and just be alone for an hour. I don't know what else to say. We're not going to settle this right now anyway . . . Okay? . . . Jake? . . . Did that go by you too?

JAKE   No. I caught it. *(She looks at him, then starts up the stairs)* . . . How much does Michael Jaffe have to do with this?

MAGGIE *(She stops, turns around)*   What?

JAKE   Michael Jaffe . . . Wrong name or just the wrong time to say it?

MAGGIE *(Nervously)*   What are you talking about?

JAKE   I'm talking about Michael Jaffe.

MAGGIE   What about him?

JAKE   Right. What about him? I know very little except he's extremely bright, that he's brought a new "energy" to your office, that everyone likes him and that things have really "perked up" since he's come to work there . . . And a jogger too, didn't you tell me that? You went jogging with him when you were all in Chicago, I believe you said. It's nice for someone like you who's always running to have someone to run with, am I right, Mag?

MAGGIE   I'm not going to get into one of these discussions.

(She turns away)

JAKE *(He snaps)* Oh, come on, Maggie, get into it. I want to know just how "perked up" things are with you two . . . Is that an unfair question to ask, seeing as it comes on the heels of you asking me for a separation? . . . Are you having an affair with him or not? *(She looks at him, speechless)* . . . No answer? Does that mean you're not having an affair with him?

MAGGIE . . . No.

JAKE No . . . So you're *not* having an affair with him.

MAGGIE No.

JAKE Alright, let me rephrase the question . . . Have you slept with him?

MAGGIE *(As if it's the last word she'll ever speak)* . . . Yes.

JAKE Yes?

MAGGIE Yes.

JAKE Jesus Christ, what did I ask that for?

MAGGIE I'm sorry, Jake.

JAKE Oh, shit, Maggie.

MAGGIE Jake—

JAKE   I was smart enough to figure it out and dumb enough to make you say it.

MAGGIE   I shouldn't have said it, Jake. The truth doesn't fix anything.

JAKE   No. It just makes it clearer.

MAGGIE   It's not an affair because it stopped as soon as it started. But it happened and I'm sorry . . . Jake? I don't think we should say anything more. We're just going to hurt each other.

JAKE   I thought we passed that a minute ago.

MAGGIE   *(She is about to go, then stops, turns to him)* Did—did you— I'm sorry. The guilt is so great, I'm trying to make it easy on myself . . . Did you ever do anything? In all the years we were married? . . . You don't have to answer it, but maybe I'd feel better if I knew . . . Did you?

   (JAKE sits there, thinking)

JAKE   . . . If I said yes, would it make any difference? About the separation?

MAGGIE   No.

JAKE   Then my answer would be meaningless, wouldn't it?

MAGGIE   Nothing we do is meaningless.

JAKE   Alright. Then I'll tell you.

MAGGIE   No . . . It doesn't really matter. Exchanging guilts isn't exactly going to save the day.

(She turns, goes upstairs and is gone. JAKE turns to the audience)

JAKE   I didn't even get the opportunity to lie . . . which I don't think I would have . . . Of all the imaginary conversations I have, ten, twenty, fifty a day, why did this have to be a real one? *(He points upstairs)* Up there I could have fixed all this. Turn on the machine and rewrite it . . . "No, Jake. There was no affair and I never slept with anyone. Michael Jaffe is a twerp . . . Don't you know you've spoiled me so, I could never let another man ever touch me" . . . Click! Turn off the processor, get a beer and turn on the Knicks–Lakers game.

(MOLLY, a twelve-year-old girl, appears and stands there. He doesn't see her but senses her presence)

JAKE   Molly? Is that you?

MOLLY   Yes, Daddy.

(JAKE turns, looks at her)

JAKE   You're so young. Eleven, twelve? Why am I thinking of you now?

MOLLY   You need someone to tell you they love you.

JAKE   That doesn't count. All little girls love their Daddies.

MOLLY Sandra Gerstein *hates* hers.

JAKE Why?

MOLLY I don't know. I made it up. I thought it would make you feel better.

JAKE No, honey. *I* made it up. Not you.

MOLLY I know. Did it make you feel better?

JAKE Yes.

MOLLY You fool yourself a lot, don't you?

JAKE You got it.

MOLLY Why are you and Maggie breaking up?

JAKE I don't know, Molly.

MOLLY Is it because you both had an affair?

JAKE Jesus, I'm not going to discuss this with a twelve-year-old.

MOLLY Then when?

JAKE When you come back like you are today. All grown up.

MOLLY Alright. I will.

(YOUNG MOLLY moves out as OLDER MOLLY, at twenty-one, appears from the opposite side)

OLDER MOLLY   So tell me, Dad.

JAKE *(To the audience)*   Gee, time flies when you're neurotic.

OLDER MOLLY   I know what's wrong with you and Maggie. It's not about Michael Jaffe *or* your actress friend.

JAKE   It's not? Then what *is* it about?

OLDER MOLLY   It's about Mom.

JAKE   Your mother's been dead for ten years.

OLDER MOLLY   I know. Ghosts are a bummer, aren't they?

JAKE *(He nods)*   *Life's* a bummer, kiddo.

OLDER MOLLY   I thought self-pity was a no-no.

JAKE   Only on the stage. In life it's very comforting.

OLDER MOLLY   Boy, do you need help, Dad.

JAKE   I didn't have to think *you* up to tell me that.

OLDER MOLLY   Why don't you talk to Edith? Come on, talk to her.

JAKE   Analysts don't work nights. That's when they have their *own* breakdowns.

OLDER MOLLY   I don't mean *really* talk to her. Make *up* that you talk to her.

JAKE   Some session. I make up Edith, the questions *and* the answers. What's the point?

OLDER MOLLY   Complete control. Your favorite thing in life.

JAKE   It isn't really. It's being at the mercy of someone else that scares me. Been that way since I was a baby. My mother was always afraid I'd fall out of my high chair so she tied me in with a rope. Couldn't move my hands, couldn't push away the baby food I hated. I had to fight her off with my nose.

OLDER MOLLY   That's awful.

JAKE   I grew up thinking that's the way life was. First time she took me to a restaurant I couldn't eat because the waiter forgot to tie me up.

OLDER MOLLY   No wonder you're in analysis.

JAKE   That was a problem too. By now I had claustro-phobia. For the first year in Edith's office, I wouldn't let her close the door. Everyone in the waiting room heard my life story. I'd walk out and someone sitting there would say, "You're sounding better today". . . Then it got worse. On airplanes I was always afraid of being locked in the john. So I kept testing the door, opening it and closing it. The sign above would light up, "Occupied, Vacant, Occupied, Vacant" . . . I think maybe that's why I became a writer. I could write when I wanted, where I wanted and what I wanted.

OLDER MOLLY   Maybe Maggie doesn't want to be tied up either.

JAKE   Smart observation.

OLDER MOLLY   So maybe you better talk to Edith.

JAKE   For you, anything. See you later, babe.

OLDER MOLLY   Anytime . . . You're on, Edith.

(OLDER MOLLY goes off just as EDITH, a woman in her late forties, comes on)

EDITH   Just what I need. A session *he* makes up that I don't even get paid for . . . So what is it this time, Mr. Creative?

(She sits on a chair. He sits on the sofa)

JAKE   Please, Edith, I'm shopping for a little compassion.

EDITH *(Like a mother to an infant)*   Ahh, wassa mawa, baby?

JAKE *(To the audience)*   She actually does that in sessions. It's the New Age analysis. Make the patient look like a schmuck.

EDITH   Is that what I'm here for, Jake? To set up straight lines for you?

JAKE   I'm lost, Edith. Confused. I had an affair with someone but I don't want to leave Maggie. She *slept* with someone and she *does* want to leave.

EDITH   So what's your point? Your affair wasn't as good as the guy she slept with?

JAKE   Forget it, Edith. You're not an analyst. You're a mother with a diploma.

EDITH   And what are you? A martyr! A self-made sufferer! Don't you know you're better than that, Jake? You're a warm, loving, giving human being with incredible sensitivity. And Maggie doesn't even appreciate that.

JAKE   You really think so?

EDITH   I don't know. They're your words, I'm just moving my lips.

JAKE   *(To the audience)*   See? I'm a schmuck again. *(To EDITH)* Edith, I need help. Real help. I'm giving you temporary freedom. Make up your own words.

EDITH   Alright. Why do you like to deprive yourself so much, Jake?

JAKE   Oh, Christ, Edith. We do that question every week. I hate that question. Don't you have another question?

EDITH   Yes. Here's one. Why don't you like me to ask you why you like to deprive yourself?

JAKE   This is my last session, Edith. Real or not. And then I'm going to find another analyst to help me understand why I went to you so long.

EDITH   Can I suggest someone? My son, Arthur, just started his own practice. It's in California, but he's worth the trip.

JAKE   God, you make me so furious. Do you know what I'd like to do to you right now, Edith?

EDITH   *(In infant talk again)*   Wha, baby? Tell mawa what Jakey wanna do?

JAKE *(To the audience)*   She could lose her license for this, you know. *(To EDITH)* I'd like to either punch your face out with my fist or rip your clothes off and hump the life out of you.

EDITH   I know what *my* choice is . . . Which do you prefer?

JAKE   Forget it. It's just wishful thinking.

EDITH   When you wish, you wish upon the child in you. Do you know who said that?

JAKE   Jiminy Cricket?

EDITH   No. Me! . . . Didn't you read my book?

JAKE   *Love Yourself, Fuck Them?* Was that the title?

EDITH   You are so naughty . . . How's your sex life, Jake?

JAKE   My sex life? You think Maggie and I are screwing eight hours a day while we discuss our breakup?

EDITH   Maybe if you did, you wouldn't be breaking up.

JAKE   Edith, I am so tired of your fortune cookie wisdom. I picture some patient coming to you with no arms, no legs, no eyes, no ears, no mouth and you asking him how his sex life is.

EDITH   Well, if he found a way to get to my office, why not?

JAKE   Edith, did you ever *actually* cure anyone?

EDITH   Analysis doesn't cure you, Jake. It just makes you feel better between sessions.

JAKE   You know, I should have married you instead of Maggie. Then I wouldn't be so unhappy about the marriage breaking up.

EDITH   You know what I think, Jake? And listen to this because I think I'm going to say something very profound.

JAKE   Oh, good. *60 Minutes* will be one hour late tonight in order to bring you this CBS Special, "Edith Reports." And now, Dr. Edith Hassenberg.

EDITH *(Out front)* Thank you, Don, and good evening. *(To JAKE)* I'll tell you what I think. I think you won't hit me so you can deprive yourself of anger and you won't hump me so you can deprive yourself of loving. And then you make fun of it so you can deprive yourself of feelings.

JAKE How did you work that out?

EDITH Easy. You're a Sagittarius.

JAKE You'd better let me have your son's number . . . You—are—ludicrous.

EDITH You make Karen foolish and you make me ludicrous! Is this your way of getting back at women because Julie died and Maggie stands up to you?

JAKE I'm handling this the best way I can . . . I have one dead wife and one on the way out the door. What do you want, a tap dance?

EDITH Why not? You're unhappy if you want to be. You're lonely if you want to be. It's your choice.

JAKE My choice that Julie died? That Maggie's leaving?

EDITH I didn't say your fault. I said your choice.

JAKE I don't get it.

EDITH If you want to suffer, you suffer. If you want to be fat, you're fat. We make our own destiny, Jake.

JAKE   Is that why you're still unmarried?

EDITH   No. Most men are shits. *(He walks away, throwing his hands up)* Oh, this is pointless, Jake. Do you want the Comedy Store or do you want help? Don't mock me, use me.

JAKE   Okay. Alright. What do you want?

EDITH   Answers. *Real* answers. If you could have anything you wanted in the world, right now, this minute, this second, what would you ask for?

JAKE   Don't do this to me, Edith.

EDITH   Answer me, Jake. What would you ask for?

JAKE   You *know* what I would ask for.

EDITH   Then say it.

JAKE   Stop it. STOP IT!

EDITH   Ask for it, then I'll stop it . . . Ask for it, Jake. Please!

JAKE   JULIE! . . . I WANT JULIE!

(Suddenly, JULIE appears, a lovely young girl about twenty-one, in jeans and a shirt, lying on a bench with the New York Times Magazine *and a pen)*

JAKE sees her and moves toward her)

JAKE   I want her alive, the way I remember her. I want
to be twenty-four when she was twenty-one. I want to
be lying on the grass in Central Park on a Sunday
morning, watching her do the *Times* crossword puzzle,
knowing the first true happiness I ever felt in my life.

JULIE *(Without looking up)*   Jake? Who's the Iron Man of
Baseball? Nine letters.

JAKE   Lou Gehrig.

JULIE   Right. Very good. *Ninotchka* director, thirteen
letters.

JAKE   Ernst Lubitsch.

JULIE   My God, you're a genius. *(We hear bells. She turns
and looks)* Hey! There's the ice cream man. I'm buying.
What do you want?

JAKE   Chocolate. Seven letters.

JULIE   Seven letters is vanilla. You pay. I'll be right back.

(She runs off)

JAKE *(Continuing)*   . . . and I lay there, looking up at the
sky, dreaming about what the rest of our lives would
be like . . . And I want the rest of our lives . . . Can you
get me Julie, Edith?

EDITH   No.

JAKE   Then don't play games with me.

EDITH I don't play games, Jake. You do.

JAKE Yes . . . I do.

EDITH Why?

JAKE Because in games, I never lose. And what I lose, I can rewrite.

> (*MAGGIE comes out of the upstairs bathroom in a terry cloth robe. She moves to the stairs*)

MAGGIE Can we talk for a minute?

JAKE (*He looks up*) Sure . . . Would you like a drink?

EDITH No, thanks, I have to leave now.

MAGGIE Yes, please. A vodka.

> (*EDITH turns and sees MAGGIE, who has come down the stairs*)

EDITH Oh. I didn't see her. (*She moves closer to MAGGIE*) She looks beautiful. I've always loved her face. And that wonderful skin. So English and clean. I have skin like lost luggage.

> (*JAKE has moved to the bar to make MAGGIE's vodka*)

JAKE Feeling any better?

MAGGIE No. Just cleaner.

EDITH Listen to her, Jake. Hear her out. Don't say no to everything. You always have options. *(She starts to back out)* That's what life's about . . . Options . . . Options . . . I love how my voice trails off . . . Options . . . Options . . .

(She's gone. JAKE hands MAGGIE her drink)

MAGGIE How are *you* feeling?

JAKE Tired. Trauma always exhausts me.

MAGGIE . . . I'm scared, Jake. I've never been this scared in my life. Not since I left Michigan to go on my own. So here I am, seventeen years later, doing the same thing I did then and feeling the same emptiness in the pit of my stomach. I haven't made much progress, have I?

JAKE Maybe we shouldn't have married until you stopped running.

MAGGIE My fault, Jake. I thought you were the finish line . . . This isn't going to turn ugly, is it?

JAKE Maybe. I don't know. But at least I'm fighting with every goddamn thing I have to save this. What are *you* doing?

MAGGIE Trying to save this marriage the only way I know how. By giving it up for a little while.

JAKE You can't keep what you give up.

MAGGIE Why not? You did it with me for eight years.

JAKE *I* did? What did I keep?

MAGGIE Well, Julie, for one thing. She may have died but you never let go. Wherever we moved to, wherever we traveled, we always took Julie with us. Some nights I was tempted to put down an extra dinner plate for her, but I didn't think you'd be amused . . . I had to live *your* memories for so long. It was always *your* friends, *your* family, your work, as if I were a replacement, a substitute, always trying to make the first team.

JAKE The first team? Jesus, you devoted so much of this marriage trying to become chairman of the board, I never saw you for half those eight years. I don't know whose dream you were trying to fulfill, but it sure as hell wasn't mine.

MAGGIE Well, unfortunately, it wasn't mine either. For as long as I can remember, I was molded and shaped in the form of somebody *else's* concept of a woman, never mine. The church taught it to me, parochial schools taught it to me, my mother, my father—God, you couldn't get out of the Midwest without its stamp of approval. I was taught to be a good girl, a wife and a mother but never a person. You could be a carbon copy but don't mess with being an original. That's what you married eight years ago, Jake. A good girl. As good and as obedient as my mother, never suspecting, of course, that it was three martinis a day that kept her obedient . . . And then one day I woke up and said to myself, "I don't want to be anyone's concept of me except me . . . not even Jake's" . . . You are so important to me, but you're also so consumed with creating your own images and characters, planning every detail of their life, molding them and shaping them into *your* creations, *your* concepts. And I said, "Jesus, I just left all this in Michigan, what do I want it in New York for?" ... And the minute I tried to step out on my own, to try to be someone *I* created, that *I* controlled, you made me pay so dearly for it. You made me feel like a plagiarist ... And so one day in Chicago, I let myself become a very bad little girl. The next morning I looked in the mirror and I sure didn't like what I saw. But I saw the possibility of becoming someone who would have to be accepted on *her* terms and certainly not someone who was considered a rewrite of someone else. And until you begin to see *me*, Jake, *my* Maggie, I am getting out of this house, out of this life and out of your word processor ... I may be making the biggest mistake of my life but at least it'll be mine . . . Dear Lord, Creator of the Universe, forgive me. And if not, not.

JAKE . . . You're not assuming I'm the Creator of the Universe, are you?

MAGGIE No, Jake, but thanks for telling me . . . I'm leaving. Give us both a break and don't fight it.

JAKE Fight what? You've made up your mind.

MAGGIE There were two of us in the ring, Jake. I'll try to move some of my things out tomorrow.

JAKE Tomorrow? Then we still have an interesting night ahead of us.

MAGGIE   I'm not staying tonight. I thought I'd drive out
to the beach house. Is that alright with you?

JAKE   It's your house too.

MAGGIE   Thank you.

JAKE   I'll keep the half facing the ocean.

MAGGIE   This is going to be hard on Molly.

JAKE   She's a strong kid. She'll be alright.

MAGGIE   Still, it's the second time she's losing a mother
. . . and the third time I'm losing a child. Maybe that's
why she means so much to me.

JAKE   I wanted those babies as much as you, Maggie.
Maybe things might have been different for us.

MAGGIE   Maybe. But as bad as those two nights in the
hospital were, I thought that was the closest we've ever
been to each other.

JAKE   We didn't get any breaks, did we?

MAGGIE   Will you be here tomorrow?

JAKE   To watch you pack? No, thanks. I'll spare myself
that. I've always hated the sight of a wife leaving.

MAGGIE   Then there isn't much left to say, is there?

JAKE   I guess not.

MAGGIE *(She starts up the stairs, but stops at the top)*   Jake! I know nothing in life ever hurt you as much as Julie dying . . . Well, tonight is the worst thing that's ever happened to me.

(She leaves)

JAKE *(To the audience)*   I haven't hung on to Julie . . . I swear to you, I have tried over and over and over to get Julie out of my mind. I *never* summon her up. She just bursts in on me.

(JULIE, still at twenty-one, but dressed differently, bursts in on him)

JULIE *(Angrily)*   Where were you?

JAKE   When?

JULIE   Last night. This morning. Right now. This minute. How could you not call me? How could you not want to know how I feel?

JAKE   About what?

JULIE   About *what?* About what happened to us.

JAKE   I don't know. What happened to us?

JULIE   Oh, my God. I don't believe this.

JAKE   Julie, I had a *very* busy day. People in and out of here. I'm sorry . . . What happened to us?

JULIE *WE MADE LOVE!*

JAKE We did?

JULIE "We did," he says. We slept together. For the first time, Jake. Not just *our* first time. It was *my* first time . . . ever! And you don't remember it?

JAKE Oh, *that* first time. Yes. I do. I just didn't realize you were going back twenty-nine years.

JULIE I'm not going back twenty-nine years. I'm going back to last night.

JAKE I know. I know.

JULIE Well, aren't you going to ask me how I feel?

JAKE Sure. How do you feel, Julie?

JULIE *(Exasperated)* Forget it. Never mind. It doesn't matter.

JAKE No, it does, Julie. I swear. It's just that it comes at a bad time. Maggie's upstairs getting ready to leave me.

JULIE Who's Maggie?

JAKE My second wife.

JULIE Well, she can be your first wife for all I care because I'm not sure you and I are ready for marriage.

JAKE   Julie, please don't mix up my time periods. It confuses me. I'm a writer, not a computer.

JULIE   You're a writer? You go to law school.

JAKE   Yes, *then*. But later I gave up law school and became a writer.

JULIE   Really? What did you write?

JAKE   Well, you wouldn't have heard of them because I didn't write them yet. I mean, I did write them but I just thought of you *now* and you're here before they would have been written. In other words, if you were here *later*—

JULIE   Alright. I get it. I got it. Okay. God!

JAKE   You *do* get it?

JULIE   I *said* I did. I get it.

JAKE   How old are you?

JULIE   Twenty-one.

JAKE   And how old am I?

JULIE   Twenty-four.

JAKE   No, you don't get it . . . Look at me, Julie. Closely.

   (She looks at him closer)

JULIE Oh!

JAKE See what I mean?

JULIE You're in your mid-thirties.

JAKE I wish . . . Look closer, Julie. At the gray in my hair, at my skin, in my eyes.

JULIE *(She looks him over)* Oh, God, Jake. You're *old*! . . . You're my father's age.

JAKE *(Annoyed)* No, I'm not. He was fifty-eight then. I'm only fifty-three.

JULIE You're fifty-three? . . . And I slept with you last night?

JAKE It wasn't last night. It was twenty-nine years ago . . . You see when I bring you back—

JULIE Okay okay okay, I get it.

JAKE Why? Do you think I look awful?

JULIE No, not *awful* . . . Mature! . . . Look, it's okay. It happens.

JAKE Am I that different?

JULIE Well, you're a little—bulkier . . . Is that the wrong word?

JAKE You can't imagine.

JULIE   I do like the little wrinkles around your eyes
. . . and under them. It gives you—character. It's nice.

JAKE   Stick around, you'll love senility and arthritis.

JULIE   I don't care how old you are, Jake. Last night was
still wonderful. God, I was scared. That I wouldn't like
it. That *you* wouldn't like it. Did you know that out of
all my girlfriends, I'm the last one to do it? It's just that
there was never a boy I wanted to get that close to.
Never . . . But when we walked home last night, I said
to myself, if he tries, if he even puts a hand on my
shoulder, he's going to know just how much love I
have to give him . . . And it was easier than I thought
it would be, Jake . . . It was *won*derful. I am *so* glad we
picked each other because I could never be with anyone else and neither could you. You know that, don't
you?

JAKE   Julie, don't.

JULIE   Is that the wrong thing to say?

JAKE   Wrong? You make me want to hear more. To say
more. To crawl in that place you're in now and stay
there forever. But I can't do it. We're not *in* the same
place, Julie.

JULIE   We're not? *Now* I'm confused . . . Is this some sort
of dream?

JAKE   Yes. For me . . . It's a memory, Julie. You're the
memory and I'm the present. And there's no future.
Not a *real* future. Because we can never be together the

way we once were. In life, I mean . . . That life is gone
. . . Can you understand what I'm saying?

JULIE   Oh, God . . . Oh, my God, Jake . . . Are you dead?

JAKE *(Exasperated)*   Jesus!

JULIE   Oh, Jake, I'm so sorry. When did it happen? Was
it terrible? Well, of course, it would *have* to be terrible.
No wonder you look older. They say your whole life
flashes in front of you just before you die. That would
age somebody, wouldn't it?

JAKE *(To the audience)*   I haven't got the heart to tell her.

(To KAREN)

JAKE   Karen, help me.

(KAREN rushes out)

KAREN *(Upstairs)*   What is it, Jake?

JAKE   She thinks *I'm* the one who died. What'll I tell
her?

KAREN   That's not for us to do, Jake. Maybe a policeman
or a rabbi.

JAKE *(To JULIE)*   It wasn't me, Julie. It was you.

JULIE   That died? Oh, I'm so relieved. I hate it when
someone I love dies.

KAREN   Such a sweet girl, but a little naive, no?

JAKE *(To KAREN)*   No. She's just young.

JULIE *(To JAKE)*   Now I see why you bring me back. It's mostly when you're in trouble, isn't it?

KAREN   Join the club, honey.

JAKE   No, not exactly—

JULIE   Yes, it's true, Jake. Every time I come here, your life's in turmoil.

KAREN   Remember the heart attack?

JULIE   I remember when you had a heart attack. I was here, wasn't I?

JAKE   Well, after you left I found out it was just a bad shrimp.

JULIE   Then why didn't you get me back here and tell me?

JAKE   Well, you were so comforting, I really enjoyed it.

(EDITH appears upstairs, on the opposite side from KAREN)

EDITH   What about that tragedy in the paper?

JULIE   And I was here the night that terrible tragedy was in the paper.

JAKE That was just a bad review in *Time* magazine
. . . Look. I panic sometimes. I admit it.

JULIE And now I'm here because Maggie is leaving you.

EDITH He uses people like Kleenex.

JAKE *(To JULIE)* There's hardly a day in my life that I
don't think of you, Julie.

JULIE But you don't send for me unless you're in trouble. That's not fair, Jake. That's not honest. Because I
come here with such expectations. You use the beginning of the best part of my life to get you through the
worst part of yours. Make up your mind, Jake. Is this
time for me or for her?

EDITH *(To KAREN)* This is interesting. *This* is fascinat-
ing. I can't follow it but it's riveting.

JAKE *(To JULIE)* Julie, would it be alright if this time was
just for *me*? Because right this minute I don't think I
could give either one of you what you need.

JULIE If you need me now, that's alright. I'll do whatever I can. The thing is, I don't know if I can do it like
this.

JAKE Like what?

JULIE Being twenty-one. I'm too young, too inex-
perienced. How can I help you when I don't even
know what life is about yet . . . Make me older, Jake.
Make me—thirty-six.

JAKE I can't do that, Julie.

JULIE Sure you can. I want to see what I'd look like anyway. If I'm going to be fat, I'll start dieting now.

KAREN *(To EDITH)* He wants her younger. She wants to be older. Can you imagine? Only a dead woman would think like that.

JULIE I'm doing it, Jake. I'm going out. I'll see you in fifteen years. Don't go away, otherwise I can't come back.

(She starts out)

JAKE Stop it, Julie. I can't do it.

JULIE Why not?

JAKE Because . . . you never *were* thirty-six.

JULIE I wasn't? . . . Oh . . . How old did I get to be?

JAKE Thirty-five.

JULIE That's very young, isn't it?

KAREN *(To EDITH)* This is the sad part. I'm going to see what else is on.

(She leaves)

EDITH Don't make it too depressing, Jake. You just slept with the girl last night.

(She goes)

JULIE How did it happen?

JAKE Don't you remember?

JULIE No.

JAKE How can you not remember that?

JULIE Because I'm twenty-one. It hasn't happened yet . . . Tell me, Jake.

JAKE It was an auto accident. Coming back from Vermont. The end of June.

JULIE Were you in the car?

JAKE No. The night before, in Vermont, I got a call my mother was sick in Florida. I got a flight out in the morning. You drove back yourself.

JULIE What were we doing in Vermont?

JAKE We were taking Molly up to camp.

JULIE Molly?

JAKE You don't know who Molly is?

JULIE *(She shakes her head no, then realizes)* . . . Oh, God . . . We had a girl. *(JAKE nods)* When?

JAKE You were twenty-four. No, twenty-five.

JULIE *(She smiles)*   We had a baby . . . We had a little girl
. . . What is she like, Jake?

JAKE   Like you. Pretty. Smart. Impetuous . . . She's at
college now. At Amherst.

JULIE   Amherst?

JAKE   Is that alright?

JULIE   Yes. It's wonderful. Why did you pick Amherst?

JAKE   I didn't. You did. You said if we had a child, you
wanted her to go to Amherst.

JULIE   No, I said Dartmouth.

JAKE   Oh. I thought you said Amherst . . . She only has
six months left. She could transfer.

JULIE   No, no. Too much packing to do . . . So tell me
about us. Were we a happy family? What did we do in
the summers? Did we have a dog?

JAKE   Yes. A yellow Labrador.

JULIE   Perfect. What was his name?

JAKE   Bark.

JULIE   Bark?

JAKE   Yes. I asked him his name and he said—

53

JULIE *(She laughs)* Bark! Alright . . . What about the summers? Where did we go?

JAKE We rented a farmhouse in New Hampshire.

JULIE All my dreams are coming true. Was Molly a happy baby?

JAKE Oh, laughed all the time. Even in her sleep. She loved everything . . . Only kid I knew who couldn't wait to get her shots at the doctor's.

JULIE Are you exaggerating?

JAKE Well, maybe embellishing.

JULIE Oh, God. I wish we could have lived there for the rest of our lives.

JAKE We did.

JULIE *(She gets it)* Oh. Right . . . I got everything I wanted, Jake. Didn't I?

JAKE Almost.

JULIE Do you think I could see her?

JAKE Molly? Sure. There's pictures all over here. *(He opens a drawer)* I took some great ones out at the beach this summer. *(She looks at one)* Here.

JULIE Is that her? Oh, Jake . . . She looks so grown up.

JAKE *(He looks)* Well, actually she's six months older than you are now.

JULIE Not pictures, Jake. I want to see Molly.

JAKE You mean *Molly* Molly? She's not here. She's up at school.

JULIE Send for her.

JAKE Send for her? You mean call her and tell her to drive down here and see what I'm thinking?

JULIE No. Think of her too. Snap your fingers. I don't know how you do it. Just do it. I just want to see her. To talk to her.

JAKE About what?

JULIE None of your business. Mother and daughter things. Private stuff. Without you here.

JAKE Julie, if I go, my thoughts go with me. They're attached to my brain.

(The phone rings)

JULIE You owe this to me, Jake.

JAKE I do?

JULIE For making me come only when you need me. Well, now I need you.

55

(The phone rings again)

JAKE *(He picks up the phone)* Hello? . . . Oh. Molly. *(To JULIE)* It's Molly. The real Molly. *(Back into the phone)* We were just thinking about you. *I* was.

JULIE Can I listen? Can I hear her voice?

JAKE Please. AT&T is having enough trouble. *(Into the phone)* Sorry, hon. I was on long distance. How are you? How's school? . . . Oh, stop worrying. You always think you're going to fail your exams.

JULIE I was the same way. Can I tell her that?

JAKE *(Into the phone)* Molly, could you hold it one second. I want to turn down the TV. *(To JULIE)* I'll try. Another time. I promise.

JULIE On my birthday? Can I see our daughter on my birthday?

JAKE Your birthday?

JULIE Instead of a present. I don't even want a cake. Just Molly. Say yes, Jake.

JAKE Okay. Yes. I promise.

JULIE Write it on your calendar. October twelfth. Lunch with Molly and Julie.

JAKE *Lunch?* I'm not taking you two to lunch. Julie, please. Don't turn this into science fiction. Just say goodbye.

JULIE *(Backing off)* Goodbye, Jake. I love you . . . Last night was great . . . Even if it was twenty-nine years ago. See you October twelfth.

(She is gone)

JAKE *(Back into the phone)* Molly? Sorry . . . A little hectic today . . . Listen, hon. There's a little trouble here . . . No, no . . . Domestic . . . Can we talk about it later? . . . Thanks . . . Maggie's upstairs . . . Listen, don't tell her I said anything . . . I love you too . . . Hold on. *(He presses another button, then talks into the phone)* Hi. It's Molly. Do you want to talk to her? . . . No, I just said there were problems but I didn't go into any details . . . I think so too . . . Alright. Hold on. *(He switches buttons again, then hangs up. He looks up at the audience. To the audience)* Molly knew what was wrong without me even telling her. She knew me better than I knew myself . . . I have a theory that wisdom doesn't come with age. It comes at childhood, peaks around eighteen, then slides slowly down the scale into adulthood . . . Parents express anger at a child by saying, "You ungrateful little brat. You'll never amount to anything" . . . But kids are creative. They express anger by going to school and drawing a picture of you with the head of a gargoyle . . . God has protected children with a purity of spirit and the ability to see things as they really are. They have an uncanny knack for speaking simple truths . . . Molly, as young as she is, had the one quality I was never able to find, or worse still, never able to accept in another human being . . . Trust! *(He goes to the other side of the stage)* For example, on the first day when she and Maggie met eight years ago, as certain as I was about Maggie, it was Molly alone whose stamp of approval I needed. I remember it as if it were yesterday.

(He snaps his fingers.

MAGGIE comes on. This is MAGGIE eight years ago. Her clothes are less fashionable but her eagerness is infectious. She carries a gift-wrapped book and a wet floppy hat that is crushed and dirty)

MAGGIE   I'm late, I know. I'm sorry.

JAKE   What is it?

MAGGIE   A bus went by and blew my hat off. I chased it five blocks all the way downtown . . . And then a cab ran over it and dragged it back *up*town . . . And by the time I got it, a dog was chewing on it. I bought it just for tonight. I wanted to look nice for your daughter. I wanted to make a good impression on her.

JAKE   Then wear it. That's the way *she* dresses.

MAGGIE   Don't make fun of me, Jake. Tonight is important . . . I bought her a book. Does she like books?

JAKE   Loves books. What did you get her?

MAGGIE   I don't know.

JAKE   You don't know?

MAGGIE   No. I was rushing in the store. I didn't want to be late, so I just grabbed a book in the children's section and had them wrap it up.

JAKE   She'll love the book and she'll love you.

MAGGIE   Maybe I'm trying too hard to please her. Listen, maybe there's a chance I won't like *her*.

JAKE   That's right. Maybe you won't.

MAGGIE   What would you do?

JAKE   Well, as soon as your hat dried, I'd ask you to leave.

MAGGIE   You wouldn't.

JAKE   Of course I wouldn't. It's a joke.

MAGGIE   Don't ever kid me, Jake. I have absolutely no sense of humor.

JAKE   Don't worry. We'll get you a tutor.

MAGGIE   You will?

JAKE   No. That's a joke, too.

MAGGIE   So where's Polly?

JAKE   Molly. She's inside, trying on every outfit in her closet.

MAGGIE   Where are we going to eat?

JAKE   Sung Foo's. It's Szechuan Chinese. Her absolute favorite.

MAGGIE Oh, God. Sung Foo's. I got sick there once.

JAKE Okay, we'll go somewhere else.

MAGGIE No, I don't want to disappoint her. We'll go. I'd rather get sick.

JAKE Good. Get sick. She'd love that.

MAGGIE Why?

JAKE She wants to be a doctor.

MAGGIE Okay, now *that* was a joke.

JAKE No, it wasn't.

MAGGIE Damn, they're so hard to spot.

JAKE She's going to love you, Maggie. I promise.

MAGGIE God, I hope so, Jake.

JAKE You don't have the slightest idea of how special you are, do you?

MAGGIE Oh, please don't say that, Jake. I have trouble taking compliments.

JAKE Didn't your parents ever give them to you?

MAGGIE Please. I graduated from high school second in my class and for a year my father called me his "little runner-up."

JAKE I'm sorry.

MAGGIE Our backgrounds are so different, Jake. I wish I were born in New York, like you. Everyone's so talkative, so open here. You and Julie had so much in common, I know. Maybe that's why I'm nervous about Molly. I can picture being your wife but will she want me as a mother?

JAKE Why don't you just start out as friends and the rest will take care of itself.

MAGGIE You're smart, you know that? Well, of course, you know it. I have to be told. But I know we're good for each other, Jake. You and I must have come together for some important reason. And you're what I want, what I need. Someone to center my life on. Sometimes I run on supercharged batteries and if you don't watch me, I could spin right out into another galaxy.

JAKE Perfect. Because my head is in the clouds most of the—

(*Before he can finish, she kisses him. He puts his arms around her.*

MOLLY, at twelve, comes out. She stops when she sees them, embarrassed)

MOLLY Oh. Hi. I'm sorry.

MAGGIE *(Nervously)* Hi . . . I must be Maggie.

JAKE *(To MOLLY)*   She's got a very quick sense of humor.

MAGGIE *(She extends her hand to MOLLY)*   I'm real glad to meet you, Sally.

MOLLY   Molly.

> *(They shake hands)*

MAGGIE   Molly. Sorry . . . *(She sits, followed by MOLLY)* So, your dad tells me you go to school at Walton.

MOLLY   Dalton.

MAGGIE   Dalton. Right . . . I went to high school in East Lansing, Michigan. And then I went to Michigan State.

MOLLY   Right. What did you major in?

MAGGIE   Political science . . . I wanted to become a political scientist . . . or something like that . . . And then I switched to premed . . . which led to advertising.

MOLLY   Right.

JAKE   Sort of like throwing darts, wasn't it?

MAGGIE *(She looks at JAKE)*   Yes, wasn't it? *(To MOLLY)* Have you thought about where you want to go to college?

MOLLY   Mm-hmm. Amherst. Dad says my mother always wanted me to go to Amherst.

MAGGIE   Oh. Good school. Good sports program. Do you play sports?

MOLLY   Not well.

MAGGIE   Me neither. Although I was a cheerleader in high school. But I depressed everyone so they let me go.

MOLLY *(She laughs)*   That's funny.

MAGGIE   It *is*? Oh, thank you, Molly. That means so much to me.

JAKE   Why don't you give Molly her present?

MAGGIE   I'll give it to her when I'm good and ready. *(To MOLLY)* I have a present for you, Molly. *(She gets the book and gives it to her)* I hope you like it.

MOLLY *(She feels it)*   It's a book, isn't it?

MAGGIE   I'm hoping it is, yes.

MOLLY   Should I open it now?

MAGGIE   Please. The suspense is killing me.

(MOLLY tears off the wrapping paper and looks at the book)

MOLLY *(Reading the title)*   The 1981 World Atlas.

(MAGGIE looks at JAKE. JAKE looks at the ceiling)

MAGGIE *(To MOLLY)* Did you read it?

MOLLY No.

MAGGIE Oh. Well, I hear it's very good.

JAKE Universal bought the movie rights.

MAGGIE *(To MOLLY)* It's a dumb choice, isn't it? I'll be honest. I grabbed it without even looking.

MOLLY No, I really need this for school because the names of the countries are changing all the time. *(She opens the book, looks at the pages)* This is terrific.

MAGGIE *(To JAKE)* See! She loves it.

JAKE You certainly know how to grab a book . . . Is anyone beside me hungry?

MAGGIE So starved you wouldn't believe it. Can we go to my favorite favorite place? Sung Foo's?

MOLLY That's my favorite favorite too.

JAKE What a small world small world this is.

MOLLY Oh! Sung Foo's was in the paper last week. Three men were killed there.

MAGGIE Really? What were they eating?

MOLLY *(Puzzled)* . . . No. They were shot.

64

Alan Alda *(left)* as Jake with Helen Shaver as Maggie.

All photos of the 1992 Broadway production at the Neil Simon Theatre by Martha Swope.

Alan Alda *(left)* as Jake with Kate Burton as Julie.

Alan Alda *(left)* as Jake with Talia Balsam *(center)* as Sheila
and Helen Shaver *(right)* as Maggie.

Alan Alda *(center)* as Jake with Kate Burton *(left)* as Julie
and Tracy Pollan *(right)* as Molly.

MAGGIE   Shot?

JAKE   It's not on the menu. You have to ask for it . . . Are we ready to go, guys?

MOLLY   I just have to turn off my TV. *(To MAGGIE)* Is it alright if I call you Maggie?

MAGGIE   Maggie? Sure, that's the only name I got right.

MOLLY *(She laughs)*   I love your humor.

(She runs off)

MAGGIE   Oh, Jake. We like each other. And I'm crazy about her. I want more, just like her . . . What a terrific day. What a terrific opportunity for all of us . . . Oh! Where's the bathroom? I forgot to go today. I am so happy.

(JAKE points, and MAGGIE rushes off. MOLLY comes back on)

MOLLY   I'm ready.

JAKE   Come here. I want to talk to you . . . The truth now. Do you like her?

MOLLY   She is the absolute best most perfect one you ever brought home. I mean *some* of them were really doozies.

JAKE   I didn't ask for an in-depth review of my social life . . . What do you like about her?

65

MOLLY   Everything. She's fun and she's pretty and she dresses nice and she's very smart. I can tell.

JAKE   How can you tell?

MOLLY   I spoke to her.

JAKE   That's right. You did . . . So do you think I should be—you know . . .

MOLLY   Serious?

JAKE   Serious about her?

MOLLY   No.

JAKE   No?

MOLLY   I think you should just marry her. This week. I can't wait for her to move in.

JAKE   What's the rush?

MOLLY   She might change her mind.

JAKE   Hey! I'm the catch of the year.

MOLLY   I know. But the years go by fast.

JAKE   Oh, thanks.

(The telephone rings inside)

MOLLY   That's my phone. I'll be right back.

(She starts to go)

JAKE   Molly? What's the absolute best thing about her?

MOLLY   That she'll make us all a good family again.

JAKE   Thank you, Molly. That's a nice thing to say.

(Her phone rings again)

MOLLY   If you two elope, can I go too?

JAKE   Sure. Bring your friends. I'll get a bus.

MOLLY   Oh, great. I will.

(She turns and runs off into her room. JAKE sits there a moment, happy.

There is another light change and MAGGIE comes out of the upstairs bathroom wearing a raincoat, a scarf on her head, and carrying a small suitcase. She looks bleak, and she sees JAKE)

MAGGIE   I didn't tell Molly too much, but she senses what's going on . . . She's driving into town on Saturday. We'll have lunch. *(She's downstairs by now)* I told the service to hold my calls. I don't think I'll go into work this week . . . I'm not even sure that job is the right thing for me now anyway. *(She starts for the door)* . . . Can I call you from the beach?

JAKE   If you like.

MAGGIE   God, I just don't know how to get through that door.

JAKE   Would you like me to open it?

MAGGIE   No. If I can get through that, I can get through anything . . . Goodbye, Jake.

JAKE   I hope not, Maggie.

(She looks over at JAKE, then goes. JAKE sits, looking morose . . . YOUNG MOLLY and OLDER MOLLY come on together)

OLDER MOLLY   Hi, Dad.

YOUNGER MOLLY   Hello, Daddy.

JAKE   *(He looks at them)*   Well! I never saw the both of you together before! . . . Any more Mollys coming? Like Molly at twelve months?

YOUNGER MOLLY   No. Molly couldn't talk at twelve months.

JAKE   And you figure I feel like talking now, right?

OLDER MOLLY   Or not talking. Whatever you want, Dad. We just want to stay and keep you company.

(They sit with him, one on either side)

JAKE   I may be sitting here all night. Maybe all week.

OLDER MOLLY   We don't mind.

YOUNGER MOLLY   We could play games. How about Actors and Actresses?

OLDER MOLLY   He doesn't want to play games now.

JAKE   No, no. That's alright. Maybe it'll take my mind off things . . . I'll go first . . . M.L. English actress.

OLDER MOLLY   Maggie Leighton.

JAKE   Right . . . M.S. Another English actress.

OLDER MOLLY   Maggie Smith.

JAKE   Right . . . The lead in *Cat on a Hot Tin Roof?*

YOUNGER MOLLY   Maggie the Cat.

JAKE   Right . . . This wasn't such a good idea, was it?

ALL THREE   No.

JAKE   No . . . Maybe just sitting quietly is the best idea.

YOUNGER MOLLY   Yes, Daddy.

(He holds their hands)

JAKE   Thank you, Molly . . . You too, Molly . . . We got through this once . . . We'll get through it again . . .

(They sit quietly, looking at him)
Curtain

Act Two

About six months later.

JAKE is sitting at his word processor. He types, then leans back in thought.

MAGGIE enters, wearing the same clothes she left in at the end of Act One, carrying the same overnight bag.

She stands there looking up at him. He sees her.

JAKE   . . . Forget something?

MAGGIE   Yes . . . Our marriage.

JAKE   I thought you packed it when you left.

MAGGIE   I thought so too. Apparently I was wrong . . . about a lot of things.

JAKE   I thought you were pretty clear about what you wanted.

MAGGIE   I found out what I wanted wasn't out there . . . I missed you, Jake. I missed the little things. The way you stare at the ceiling when you're lost in thought. The way you always find the right words to say even in the most painful situation. And I fumble through, tripping over my own tongue, trying to say to you that I was wrong. Wrong about everything. And praying to God that you haven't rented out my half of the bed or that somebody else's soap isn't sitting up there in my soap dish.

JAKE   Do you mean it, Maggie? Is that what you really want?

MAGGIE   Oh, yes, Jake, yes. Oh, God, yes. *(And suddenly*

she starts to laugh) I'm sorry, Jake. *(She laughs again)* I don't mean to laugh. But honestly, this is the *dumbest* scene you've ever written in your life.

JAKE *(Angrily)* I didn't write it. I'm just *thinking* of it.

MAGGIE Oh, good. Then you didn't waste any paper.

(This really breaks her up)

JAKE What I wasted was even *thinking* about you . . . Go on. Get out of here. I have important work to do.

MAGGIE *(Still laughing)* Don't lose the line about somebody else's soap in my soap dish. *(She picks up her bag, holding her sides laughing as she heads out)* Oh, God. I needed a good laugh.

(She is gone)

JAKE *(To the audience)* What you just witnessed is a man at the end of his rope . . . with nothing to hold on to because his wife took the rope with her . . . I don't know, I used to fantasize lust, romance, power. Now I'm into humiliation. It was six months since Maggie left and I haven't written a single word worth processing. To tell you the truth, I miss Maggie . . . Not that I haven't been dating now and then. Man does not live by abstinence alone . . . But recently, here in the privacy of my home, my mind and my thoughts, I was visited by a new and fresher hell than my warped imagination could ever dream of . . . No longer did I summon up the Karens and Ediths and Mollys of my life

to help brighten up the endless sleepless nights . . .
Now they came on their own. Uninvited. Unsum-
moned. Unstoppable.

(KAREN appears)

KAREN   Jake, could I speak to you for a minute?

JAKE   Karen, I didn't send for you. Please go away. Isn't
there an Ingmar Bergman festival somewhere?

KAREN   I just came from one. But in the middle of *Cries
and Whispers,* I began to worry about you.

JAKE   Everyone who sees *Cries and Whispers* gets worried. Well, stop it because I'm fine.

KAREN   You're not fine. You need rest. You're over-
wrought, overworked, underweight. How can you
sleep, running around like a lunatic with every woman
you bump into?

JAKE   I am not running around with every woman I
bump into. I'm very selective.

KAREN   Sure. If they're a woman, you select them. Like
that new one. That—Sheila woman.

JAKE   Don't say "That Sheila Woman." I hate that expression. It sounds like a bad television series.

KAREN   I only use that expression because I can't keep up
with all your women.

JAKE   Four! Four women in six months . . . Peggy, Kathy, Dana, Myra and Sheila . . . Five! Five women in six months.

KAREN   Susan wasn't a woman?

JAKE   Two nights. That lasted two nights.

KAREN   So what does that make her? Half a woman?

JAKE   It makes her someone I wasn't interested in.

KAREN   You go out with women you're not interested in?

JAKE   You have to go out with them before you find out you're not interested, don't you?

KAREN   You can't tell right away? *I* can.

JAKE   Good. Then *you* go out with her. If you have a good time, let me know and *I'll* go out with her.

KAREN   Why is it whenever I try to help you, you push me away? You're that way with *all* women. You're so—so—standoffish.

JAKE   *I'm* standoffish with women? I'm a thousand times more comfortable with women than I ever am with a man. I love being around them. I never even *think* of a man. Watch! . . . I'm thinking of Pop. Of Uncle Josh. Of my best friend, Marty . . . Do you see a man in here? No! . . . I happen to love women. That's my trouble. I can't seem to exist without them.

KAREN What you love is to *love* women. You love to
have women in love with you. You even love to love
women who love you because you're standoffish. But
intimacy, aha, *that* you're afraid of.

JAKE *(Incredulous)* What?

KAREN I said, "Aha, *that* you're afraid of." I think you're
afraid to lose control in a relationship with a woman.
To let a woman in so close, so deep inside of you, that
she'll gobble you up and you'll lose whatever you think
you are. You always have to be the Master, Jake. The
Master, the Conductor, the Director and the Attorney
General. You don't think it's strange that you sit
around here thinking about women and making up
what they say to you? And then you think up that *we*
make up that we come over here on our own? Come
on! How much more control do you want? . . . They
love you, they leave you, they come back to you, they
worry about you, they die, they live, they grow up,
they fall down, they fight for you, they cry for you—
it's a three-ring circus in here and all the horses and
lions and elephants are women . . . You're the star of
the show, Jake. You're the one they shoot out of a
cannon and you fly around the tent with an American
flag in your mouth and all the women go crazy and
faint and they take them away to hospitals . . . The
trouble is—it's very hard to get close to a man who's
flying around in a tent with a flag in his mouth. That's
what I call trouble with intimacy.

JAKE I couldn't be more intimate with women. I'm an
open book. I tell them everything. My feelings, my
hurts, my pains, my vulnerabilities. My intimacy scares

77

them, if you want to know the truth. And if I'm the ringmaster of the circus, how come all the acts are leaving? Mom is gone, Julie is gone, Maggie's left, Molly's on her own, Peggy, Kathy, Dana, Myra, none of those worked out. That's why you're here seven days a week. There's no one left for me. This house used to be filled with people laughing, living, loving . . . and now it's just me talking to you telling me what I'm telling you to say . . . You think I'm crazy, don't you?

KAREN   Well, you're in a peculiar line of work, Jake.

(*EDITH appears*)

EDITH   He picked it because he likes to deprive himself.

JAKE *(To EDITH)*   Who asked you? If this is a session, Edith, I'm not paying for it. Charge it to Karen.

EDITH *(To JAKE)*   Have you seen Maggie since she's back from Europe? I hear she looks beautiful.

JAKE   How would I know where Maggie is? You think that's all I have on my mind? I happen to be seeing someone now, Edith.

EDITH   Who?

KAREN   That Sheila woman.

EDITH   Well, I know for a fact that you dialed Maggie's number last night, got scared and hung up on the first ring.

JAKE *I* hung up? Jesus, even discussing a confidential thing like that in front of my sister is the most unethical goddamn thing I ever heard.

KAREN *(To EDITH)* I think he should get away. He could make believe he was in Paris for two weeks.

(JAKE looks at himself in the imaginary mirror)

JAKE My God, I can see them in the mirror. They're really here.

EDITH *(To KAREN)* I'm just trying to point out to him that he's going to keep turning down every woman he meets until he lets go of the past.

JAKE Excuse me, girls. I'm going to the bathroom.

(He walks away)

KAREN And I'm saying if he took the time to meet the right woman, he wouldn't turn her down.

EDITH The trouble is, he wouldn't know who the right woman is if he—

(On that word, JAKE goes into the bathroom and closes the door. EDITH and KAREN stop talking. They don't freeze, but they have nothing to say without JAKE there.

Finally, we hear the toilet flush and JAKE comes out of the bathroom)

EDITH —met her, for God sakes.

(JAKE picks up the phone and starts to dial)

EDITH *(To JAKE)* Who are you calling?

JAKE I'm calling you!

EDITH *(She looks at her watch)* At four-twenty? I'm with a patient.

JAKE I pity whoever it is. *(Into the phone)* Hello? Edith?

EDITH That's not me. It's my answering machine. Wait for the beep.

JAKE *(He waits, listening)* Christ! Do I have to listen to the entire album of *Man of La Mancha?*

EDITH *(She looks at her watch)* . . . Okay! *Now!*

JAKE *(Into the phone)* Edith. It's Jake. I'm at home. I'm having one of those things we talked about. This time it's you and my sister. Could you call me on your break? Please, just call me back as soon as you can.

(He hangs up)

EDITH *(To KAREN)* By the way, Karen. I think I met a man. Very attractive, very wealthy, recently widowed. As a matter of fact, he's the patient I'm having the session with right now.

KAREN Isn't it unethical to date your own patient?

EDITH   Yes. But if this thing gets serious, I'll tell him he's cured.

JAKE *(Exasperated)*   Christ Almighty! *(The phone rings. He quickly picks it up)* Hello? . . . Yes, Edith. Thanks for calling back. Yes, they're sitting in here now. You and Karen. Dissecting me like a frog in biology . . . And Karen just made a twelve-minute speech about me being a ringmaster and flying around a circus tent with a flag in my mouth.

KAREN *(To JAKE)*   Tell her the whole speech. It was wonderful.

EDITH *(To KAREN)*   Shh. He's talking to me.

JAKE *(Into the phone)*   No, no. This is real. I can even see them in the mirror. In the beginning it just used to be my thoughts. Like when I'm writing. But now I can see them. I hear them. I can smell their perfume.

KAREN *(To EDITH)*   Some crap he must have me wearing.

JAKE *(Into the phone)*   It scares me, Edith. Does it scare you?

EDITH   No, Jake. It doesn't scare me.

JAKE *(To EDITH)*   *Will you let me talk to you,* for God sakes? *(Back into the phone)* Excuse me, Edith . . . It's driving me nuts. I have to get rid of them. My sanity is at stake here. What should I do? . . . Please tell me . . . Yes? . . . Uh-uh . . . Uh-huh . . .

81

KAREN *(To EDITH)*   I hope this isn't going to be like *Ghostbusters.*

JAKE *(Into the phone)*   Alright. If I have to, I have to. Thank you, Edith. Goodbye.

(He hangs up and starts up the stairs)

EDITH *(To JAKE)*   Where are you going?

JAKE   Upstairs. To take a bunch of Seconals. If you won't leave, at least I can *sleep* you away.

(He starts up again)

EDITH   Jake, no. You'll kill yourself.

JAKE *(He points to the phone)*   It was your suggestion.

EDITH   It *was?*

KAREN *(As she goes)*   Pills! Pills! That's all you doctors know . . . Then what does he need a psychiatrist for?

EDITH   Who else is going to get him the pills?

(They are both gone)

JAKE *(He turns to the audience)*   You want to know how low I've sunk? *(He points to the phone)* I never spoke to Edith. I called my service. I actually made a phone call pretending I was speaking to the *real* Edith to scare the Edith and Karen in my head out of here . . . I tricked myself and I fell for it . . . The thing about going crazy is that it makes you incredibly smart, in a stupid sort of way. *(He moves toward the audience)* But I do feel like I'm losing a grip on myself. As if I'm spiraling down in diminishing circles like water being drained from a bathtub, and suddenly my big toe is being sucked down into the hole and I'm screaming for my life . . . No. Not my life. My mother . . . Why, tell me why, it's always your mother. It's never your father or an uncle or a second cousin from Detroit . . . I was five years old in a third-floor apartment in the Bronx, waking up from a nap and there's no one there. My mother is on the *fourth* floor visiting a neighbor. I'm terrified. Why doesn't she hear me? Why doesn't she come? And by the time she comes, it's too late. Your basic Freudian mother abandonment trauma has set in like cement . . . I never trusted her again. *(The intercom buzzes)* What was that? . . . Oh, the buzzer . . . God, I'm a bundle of nerves . . . *(He picks it up)* Yes? . . . Oh, Sheila . . . What a surprise, Sheila . . . Where are you, Sheila? . . . Oh, of course. Downstairs . . . Sure. Come on up, Sheila. *(To the audience)* But is Jake doomed? Not by a long shot. There's Sheila. Another woman to the rescue . . . Another woman . . . It's always another woman . . . Stop it, Jake . . . You can handle it, Jake. Get a hold of yourself, Jake . . . Get a grip on your-self . . .

(SHEILA appears, an attractive woman in her early thirties)

SHEILA Hi.

JAKE Sheila! Oh, Sheila, it's so good to see you. God,

I'm glad you're here. Where were you so long? I've been waiting all day for you.

SHEILA   You were?

JAKE   Of course I was. You look so good. So pretty. So sweet. So how are you?

SHEILA   Are you alright? . . . You look—discombobulated.

JAKE   No, no. I'm bobulated. I was just working.

SHEILA   You look exhausted. Have you been sleeping?

JAKE   While I work? No. You have to be awake to work . . . No, I'm just tired . . . Hungry. I forgot to eat . . . Oh, my God. I forgot our lunch date. Damnit, I'm sorry.

SHEILA   We didn't have a lunch date.

JAKE   We didn't?

SHEILA   Not today. You forgot *yesterday's* lunch date. I called you four times. You had your service on. Don't you check your messages?

JAKE   No. I didn't want to interrupt my train of thought.

SHEILA   Since yesterday?

JAKE   Well, it was a long train . . . I'm sorry, Sheila. I know I'm not making sense. Did I say bobulated?

. . . I can't get my thoughts together. My mind keeps stuttering. *Sputtering* . . . Skittering. What's the word I want?

SHEILA For what?

JAKE For when your mind makes jumps. Splintering. Scattering. Jesus, I can't think straight . . . Staggering. Stammering . . . *Faltering!*

SHEILA Stop it, Jake. Give your mind a rest.

JAKE I can't. I've been going through this thing. A writer thing.

SHEILA A block.

JAKE No, not a block. *Yes,* a block. Digressions. Distractions. Dissections . . . No, not dissections. *Delusions!*

SHEILA Delusions?

JAKE Like delusions. I veer off. I wander. I stray. I roam. I fade off into other places.

SHEILA I can see that.

JAKE You can? Oh, no, not about you. I'm so grateful for you, Sheila. I depend on you. You comfort me, you support me, you hold me together.

SHEILA I hardly see you.

JAKE Well, I've been busy. But when you *are* here,

you're so real, Sheila. I *love* that you're real. Nobody is real anymore.

SHEILA   I *try* to be real.

JAKE   Well, you look real. You smell real. You *feel* real. *(He holds her)* Oh, God! Flesh and blood. I *love* flesh and blood . . . Some people don't have it, you know.

SHEILA   Flesh and blood?

JAKE   They're superficial. You can see right through them. Oh, maybe you can see their reflection in a mirror, but they're not really there.

SHEILA   I've met people like that.

JAKE   Oh, I could introduce you to a roomful. But *you,* Sheila. You're so vivid. So colorful. So dimensional.

SHEILA   What do you mean, dimensional?

JAKE   Dimensional. You have sides. You have a left side, a right side, a front side, a back side. You have form as a person. You have matter. Good, firm, solid matter.

SHEILA   Well, I work out in a gym a lot.

JAKE   No! That kind of matter doesn't matter . . . Listen to me. You know how people come in and out of your life? In a door, out the door. This one's here, that one's here. You know that feeling?

SHEILA   I don't entertain as much as you.

JAKE   Exactly! Exactly! That's my point. You know what my trouble is, Sheila? I work too much. I don't want work to be my life. I want my life to be my life. I let so many things go by. So many things I don't do.

SHEILA   Like what?

JAKE   Like travel. I should travel a lot more.

SHEILA   I loved our trip to Quebec.

JAKE   Okay. There you are. But there's more than Quebec. There's Europe. There's Africa. There's the Middle East. Well, no, not the Middle East, but there's Japan. Have you ever been to Japan?

SHEILA   No.

JAKE   Oh, Japan is the greatest. I was there with Maggie once. And with Julie once. And once with another girl. I'd love to go with you.

SHEILA   They must know you very well there.

JAKE   Hey! There's Australia. Have you ever been to Australia?

SHEILA   No. Just here and Quebec. I don't fly too well.

JAKE   Okay. A ship. A slow boat to China. How does that sound? China? Hong Kong? The Orient?

SHEILA   When are you talking about?

JAKE Next month. Next week. How about next week?

SHEILA Go to China next week? My vacation isn't for eight months.

JAKE You could ask them. Tell them it's an emergency.

SHEILA An emergency vacation to China?

JAKE Okay, forget China. Forget Hong Kong. What about India? Bombay? Calcutta?

SHEILA I can only get a three-day weekend, Jake. I could *go* there, but I'd have to quit my job when I *got* there.

JAKE Alright. Forget Bombay. Forget Calcutta. Forget traveling . . . I'll tell you what I'd really like to do. What would really shake my life up.

SHEILA What's that, Jake?

JAKE I want to move. It's time I moved, Sheila.

SHEILA I thought you loved this place.

JAKE I *did* love it. I don't love it now. I want a new place, Sheila. A new start. A new beginning for you and me. Do you understand what I'm saying, Sheila?

SHEILA You want me to move in with you?

JAKE Yes! . . . Not *now*. Someday. Later on. In the future.

SHEILA   So what are you saying?

JAKE   I just said it. Move in with me. But not now. Someday. Later on.

SHEILA   Why does that sound negative to me?

JAKE   It's *not* a negative. It's a *positive* negative. It's a cautious enthusiasm.

SHEILA   Like an uncommitted commitment?

JAKE   No. That's an oxymoron. What I'm saying is, I love you and I want you to be with me . . . someday, somewhere, somehow.

SHEILA   This is all new to me, Jake. You never talked like this before. I know you care for me but I never thought it was about loving.

JAKE   Didn't I just say I love you?

SHEILA   Yes, but it didn't have any immediacy to it. I feel like I have to wait for a delivery date.

JAKE   Are you saying you don't know how I feel?

SHEILA   Well, I always felt like I was needed but I never felt loved. I like being needed but being loved is better.

JAKE   So what are you saying? Have I been—what? Cold to you?

SHEILA   No. Never cold. You're warm and funny and

affectionate. But you always keep your distance. An arm's length away. Sort of—standoffish.

JAKE Oh, shit.

SHEILA Did I say something wrong? Am I the first one who ever said that?

JAKE Standoffish? I don't know. I can't recall anyone ever saying it.

SHEILA Maybe standoffish is too strong. Maybe a lack of intimacy.

JAKE Can we get off this, Sheila? We're in a holding pattern here. We're not moving this along.

SHEILA Where do you want to move it to?

JAKE All I'm trying to do is move from here to there. I'm here now but I want to get to there. Do you understand that, Sheila?

SHEILA Yes. You're here but you want to get to there.

JAKE Right! Right! That's right! From here to there, that's all.

SHEILA Jake, I mean this as a constructive positive, but you seem very confused.

JAKE I'm not confused. Well, a *little* confused. I can't keep my visions focused.

SHEILA   Is it an eyeglass thing?

JAKE   No, I see fine. I see great. Why am I having trouble with this? What is it I'm trying to say?

(MAGGIE appears. SHEILA never sees her)

MAGGIE   That you're really not interested. That you're just kidding yourself.

(She goes)

JAKE   I am *not* kidding myself.

SHEILA   About what?

JAKE *(To SHEILA)*   About us. About you and me. I think we should start seeing each other on a regular basis, Sheila.

SHEILA   You mean every night?

JAKE   Yes. Every night. Well, no, not every night. A *lot* of nights. The nights that you don't have something else to do. Or *I* don't. But most nights. Can we do that?

SHEILA   I was hoping we could spend more time together.

JAKE   Oh, there are so many things we can do.

SHEILA   Like what?

JAKE   I don't know. We'll make a list. A "things we can

do together" list. Or *you* can make the list and I'll check off what I like.

SHEILA   Sure.

JAKE   And then I'm going to move. I really never liked this neighborhood anyway. A bunch of old remodeled factories, that's all it is.

(*MAGGIE appears on the opposite side of the stage*)

MAGGIE   Ah, but Jake, it has such charm.

JAKE   And it has no charm. Some people *think* it has charm but it doesn't, believe me.

MAGGIE   Why don't we ask Sheila?

JAKE   STAY OUT OF THIS!

SHEILA   I *am*. You say it doesn't have charm, I believe you.

JAKE *(To SHEILA)*   Now uptown is the place. The Upper East Side. Do you like the Upper East Side?

SHEILA   Everybody likes the Upper East Side.

MAGGIE *(To JAKE)*   I thought you liked Brooklyn Heights.

JAKE   I *do* like Brooklyn Heights.

SHEILA   I didn't say you didn't.

JAKE *(To SHEILA)* I know. I meant Brooklyn Heights is a good idea too. Great views of the river. And nobody from New York ever comes over to visit you.

MAGGIE Of course Bedford Village is beautiful.

JAKE I *know* Bedford Village is beautiful.

SHEILA Yes, I hear it is too.

JAKE *(He smiles at SHEILA)* Yes, isn't it? The leaves turning brown in the fall. There was a house on a lake up there I always dreamed of living in.

MAGGIE Why don't you go and see it, Jake?

JAKE *(To SHEILA)* You want to go and see it, Jake? . . . Sheila? Come on, Sheila. Let's go up and see it, Sheila.

SHEILA Now? It'll be dark by the time we get there.

MAGGIE You could stay at the Bedford Inn.

JAKE *(To SHEILA)* We could stay at the Bedford Inn. Then we could see the house first thing in the morning.

SHEILA Jake, I wish you could listen to yourself. You want to go to China, Japan, Australia, Calcutta. Then you want to move to the Upper East Side and Brooklyn Heights and Bedford Village. *Nobody* can change their mind that fast.

MAGGIE *He* can.

JAKE   I can.

SHEILA   Well, I can't. I'm not a writer, Jake. I'm a businesswoman. I make up my mind slowly and carefully. If I wanted to live on the Upper East Side, I would investigate the Upper East Side.

JAKE   I know.

SHEILA   And if I wanted to live in Brooklyn Heights—

JAKE   I know.

SHEILA   I would investigate—

ALL THREE   —Brooklyn Heights.

JAKE   I know.

SHEILA   Or if I wanted to live in Bedford Village—

JAKE   I know I know I know I know.

SHEILA   *(Defensive)* I'm sorry. Live where you want, Jake. I just think you should investigate one place at a time.

JAKE   I will I will I will I will! . . . I will! . . . I'm sorry. Forgive me . . . I will.

SHEILA   Can't we just go a little slower? You move in so many directions. I never know where it is you want to get to.

MAGGIE *(She points from SHEILA to herself)*   From there to here, honey.

JAKE *(To MAGGIE)*   No, it's not.

SHEILA   What's not?

JAKE *(To SHEILA)*   It's not the way I am. I don't want to go in a lot of directions. I want to live in the country. In Bedford Village.

SHEILA   You sure you wouldn't get bored in the country, Jake?

MAGGIE *(To SHEILA)*   He'd kill himself.

JAKE *(To MAGGIE)*   Will you butt out of this?

SHEILA   Listen, I don't have to talk at all.

MAGGIE *(She gets up)*   Let's take her up on that, Jake.

(MAGGIE stands behind SHEILA and mimics every word and gesture she utters, in complete unison)

SHEILA   I don't know when I'm being negative or constructive or logically positive or conventionally destructive . . . You tell me I have a front side and a back side and an inside and an outside. I have form and dimension and matter that doesn't matter. You love me, you want me to move in with you but not today, later, in the future, someday, somehow, somewhere over the rainbow . . . Then you want to get from here to there, from there to here, MAKE UP YOUR MIND, JAKE!

I CAN'T TAKE ANY MORE. MY HAIR IS STARTING TO FALL OUT.

(They finish with their arms and bodies in the same position, like the finish of a musical number)

JAKE   Alright. I'm sorry. I didn't mean it. Forgive me.

MAGGIE   Don't *beg* her, Jake.

JAKE   I'M NOT BEGGING!

SHEILA   Who *asked* you to?

(She starts to walk away)

JAKE   Don't leave, Sheila.

SHEILA   Where am I going? To Calcutta? Don't corner me. I get very nervous when I get cornered.

JAKE   I won't corner you. We should get out of here. We should go up to Bedford. Right now.

SHEILA   Alright. Fine. I'll go to Bedford. If you want to go to Bedford, I'll go.

MAGGIE   There's a lot of traffic now. You waited too long.

JAKE   Well, there's a lot of traffic now. We waited too long.

SHEILA *YOU ASKED ME TWO MINUTES AGO!*
. . . What is wrong with you, Jake?

MAGGIE Yes, what *is* wrong with you, Jake?

JAKE *(To MAGGIE)* You know goddamn well what's
wrong. It's *you!*

SHEILA Oh, it's *me*! It's *my* fault. I'm the one who wants
to take a slow boat to Brooklyn Heights. I'm the oxymoron who can't get her visions focused.

MAGGIE *(To JAKE)* How'd you like to hear that voice the
rest of your life?

JAKE *(To MAGGIE)* Will you shut up, goddammit!

SHEILA *(Nervous, she backs away)* Jake, you're making
me nervous. I've never seen you like this.

JAKE I know. I know. It's a phase. It'll go. It'll pass. It'll
stop.

SHEILA Jake, I'm calling your doctor. What's your doctor's name?

MAGGIE Edith! Let's get Edith here. Let's have a party.

JAKE *(To MAGGIE)* I'm telling you for the last time.
SHUT UP!

SHEILA What's happening, Jake?

JAKE *(To MAGGIE)* Get out! I want you out of this house
now! Do you hear me?

SHEILA *(Frightened)* Yes, I hear you.

(She backs away)

JAKE *(To SHEILA)* Don't go, Sheila. You promised to stay. I'll get rid of her. I'll call Edith. Edith will help.

MAGGIE *(To SHEILA)* Edith won't help, Sheila. I'm a prisoner in his head. Go for help.

JAKE *(To MAGGIE)* If you don't stop, I swear, I'll kill you.

SHEILA *(She backs up, screams)* Ohhhhhh!

MAGGIE *(To SHEILA)* Run, Sheila, run. That's what I did, honey.

JAKE *(To MAGGIE)* Go on. Keep talking. You'll never leave this room alive!

SHEILA *(She screams)* Oh, God! . . . Oh, my God!

(And she goes running from the apartment)

JAKE Sheila . . . Sheila!

MAGGIE That was fun, Jake. Bitchy but fun.

JAKE Why did you do that, Maggie? What was the point of it?

MAGGIE I suppose because you didn't have the guts to tell her yourself. So you made me the hit man. To dump her would be cruel and you're not cruel, Jake. So you act like a lunatic, Sheila thinks she's well out of it and you're off the hook. You never get your hands dirty, do you?

JAKE   You don't think much of me, do you, Maggie?

MAGGIE   See what I mean? You're so afraid to face who you really are, you leave me to pass judgment on you and then blame *me* for what you don't like about yourself.

JAKE   Well, since I'm making up what you say, I might as well take advantage of it.

MAGGIE   You're cute, Jake. Nuts but cute . . . Come on, leave your work upstairs where it belongs. *(She points upstairs)* That's writing—*(She points downstairs)*—this is living . . . If surgeons lived like you, they'd be cutting people up in elevators.

> *(She starts to go)*

JAKE   Where are you going?

MAGGIE   Hopefully, out of your mind. Which is where I think *you're* going.

JAKE   Then help me.

MAGGIE   How?

JAKE *(He points up to his office)*   I want to get from there to here . . . Up there I trust what I do . . . but down here, it's people I have to trust and that's hard.

MAGGIE For everybody, Jake. That's why women carry Mace in their pocketbooks.

(*She starts to move away again*)

JAKE Will I see you again?

MAGGIE I don't know. That's between you and Maggie.

(*She leaves*)

JAKE (*He turns to the audience*) I have the feeling I'm trying to put together a jigsaw puzzle that has no picture on it . . . I'm a blank, waiting to fill in who I am . . . How did I get to be this way? . . . That's not a rhetorical question. I mean, if you know, please tell me . . . Okay, Jake. Go back to the beginning. That's what Edith always says . . . Here's another Mother story . . . I'm six years old, sitting in the kitchen with my mother, watching her shell peas . . . And on the floor I see a roach . . . My mother, faster than a speeding train, takes a newspaper and splats it against the baseboard . . . "Where do roaches come from?" I ask my mother . . . "From the dirt," she answers . . . "You mean," I say, "the roaches like to live in the dirt and eat it?" . . . "No," says Mom. "The dirt turns *into* roaches" . . . And I go back into my room, lay on the bed and say to myself, "The dirt turns into roaches" . . . And the realization hits me . . . My mother is dumb . . . And I know instinctively that six years old is too soon to find out that your mother is dumb . . . Because I'm banking my whole childhood on this woman taking care of me . . . And so I decided on that day, I would never depend on anyone except myself . . . I loved my mother, but I never asked her any more questions . . . The trouble is, here I am today at the age of fifty-three, without any answers . . . Oh my God, Julie!

(JULIE suddenly appears. This is JULIE at thirty-five. She wears a skirt and a brown suede bolero jacket)

JULIE   You remembered! I didn't sleep a wink last night wondering if you were going to send for me or not.

JAKE   Of course I was.

JULIE   Maybe you heard me praying, "Please don't forget, Jake. You've *got* to think of me today" . . . And you did, didn't you, Jake?

JAKE   Yes. I guess so. Sure. I mean otherwise what would you be doing here? . . . The thing is, it's not a good time for me right now, Julie.

JULIE   Oh. Are you writing?

JAKE   I don't know. I can't tell *what* this is anymore.

JULIE   I read some of your books. Just the first few. I didn't get to the rest yet.

JAKE   Really? What did you think?

JULIE   I liked them.

JAKE   But you didn't love them.

JULIE   No. But I see each one getting a little better than the last.

JAKE   What was wrong with them?

JULIE   They weren't you. Just be you, Jake. And don't rush the endings. You always rush the endings as if you're anxious to get on with the next one.

JAKE   I know what you mean. I sort of do that with people too . . . Julie, this has been a long day for me. Do you think we could do this tomorrow?

JULIE   Tomorrow is too late, Jake. *Today* is October twelfth.

JAKE   October twelfth?

JULIE   My birthday . . . I'm thirty-five.

JAKE   Oh, God, Julie. Yes! . . .

JULIE   So what am I wearing? Where's the mirror? I want to see how you dressed me. *(She sees the imaginary wall mirror, goes over and looks at herself)* Of course. My brown suede jacket. Your favorite . . . And that little chocolate stain is gone.

JAKE   I had it cleaned. Then I gave it to Molly. She asked for it.

JULIE   I'm glad. *(She turns around, looks at herself again)* So this is thirty-five.

JAKE   Feel any different?

JULIE   No. I don't *look* much different either. I've hardly aged.

JAKE   I know. It's your birthday. I didn't have the heart.

JULIE   Damn you, Jake, will you stop controlling everything? If I'm thirty-five, make me *feel* thirty-five.

JAKE   Okay. Okay. You're thirty-five.

JULIE   *(As if hit by a bolt, she grabs her head and stomach)* Wow! That was a kick in the head . . . What does fifty-three feel like?

JAKE   The kick gets a little lower.

JULIE   *(She stands next to him, looks in the mirror)* But this looks righter. You and me. We seem more like a couple now . . . Promise me you'll live a very long time, Jake.

JAKE   Why?

JULIE   I need you to. Otherwise who'll bring me back?

JAKE   I'm not the only one who thinks of you.

JULIE   No, but you think of me the way I want to be thought of.

JAKE   Maybe I shouldn't.

JULIE   What does *that* mean?

JAKE   You're too perfect, Julie. Too beautiful, too smart, too sweet, too understanding. No other woman can hold a candle to you. They're all standing in the dark, waiting to get a compliment from me.

JULIE   Why do you do it? Was I so terrible that you don't want to see me the way I was?

JAKE   Don't you understand, Julie? When you come back, I even make *myself* better than I am. I'm charming, I'm witty, I'm romantic, I'm "cute," I'm goddamn irresistible.

JULIE   Well, don't do it to me. I don't want to be a shrine. I don't want to be a touched-up photo in a family album. I want to be me because even a memory deserves some self-respect. Otherwise I'll never know if you would have loved me if we were still together.

JAKE   Of course I would.

JULIE   No! That's the idealization. That's the fantasy. Every man's dream—his wife never grows old . . . Well, we do, Jake. And if you keep bringing me back here looking like a young Natalie Wood and acting like Sally Field in *The Flying Nun*, I'll lose respect for you. I want to be woman enough for you because if I'm not, you won't be man enough for me. If you had died before me, I would have kept you funny and loving and sexy, but I wouldn't leave out the petulant son of a bitch you can sometimes be, because I want the whole package, damnit! . . . God, it feels so good to have a little fire in me again.

JAKE *(To the audience)*   I've created Mrs. Jakenstein.

(The phone rings. He picks it up)

JULIE   Husbands and wives fight, Jake, what's wrong with that? It's normal.

JAKE *(Into the phone)*   Hello?

JULIE   It's human.

JAKE *(Into the phone)*   Maggie?

JULIE   God, we really used to go at it sometimes.

JAKE *(Into the phone)*   How are you?

JULIE   Remember the day I threw the frozen veal chop at you? Hit you right in the head and you suddenly started to—

JAKE *(To JULIE)*   Julie, could you hold it a second. It's Maggie.

JULIE   Oh. Sorry. Go ahead.

JAKE *(Into the phone)*   . . . Where have you been? . . . Ballooning in France? . . . You don't mean getting fat, do you? . . . Oh, good . . . No, I'm fine . . . Where are you? . . . Really? That's just around the corner. *(JULIE nods to him, "Yes, let her come")* Well, I was just finishing some work. *(JULIE waves at him, shakes her head, "No. Tell her to come")* Could you hold it a second, Mag? *(He covers the phone. To JULIE)* What?

JULIE   See her, Jake. Let her come. It'll be good for you.

JAKE   With *you* here? Please! I just went through that. There's a poor girl named Sheila who's probably in Montana by now.

JULIE   I'll leave when she gets here. She's the one who called, Jake. It must be important to her.

JAKE *(He looks at her, then speaks into the phone)*   Maggie? Yes, it's fine. Great . . . I'll see you in about ten minutes . . . I am too. Bye. *(He hangs up)* You really don't mind my seeing Maggie?

JULIE *(She smiles)*   No. My time will come with you again.

JAKE *(Worried)*   Why? Have you heard something? Did they mention dates or anything?

JULIE   Don't worry about it. I'm in no rush.

JAKE   Well, it was really good seeing you today. So I'll, er . . . call you soon, okay?

JULIE   Aren't you forgetting something?

JAKE   What?

JULIE   I'm waiting for my birthday present.

JAKE   Your present? Gee, I didn't get you anything.

JULIE   Yes, you did. You just haven't delivered it yet.

JAKE   What?

JULIE   Molly! . . . You promised I could meet Molly on my birthday.

JAKE   Oh, Julie. I can't do that now.

JULIE   You promised, Jake. Suppose you die? This could be my only chance. This could be Molly's only chance to meet me. You have to do it, Jake.

JAKE   But Maggie's coming up.

JULIE   In ten minutes. We can cover a lot in ten minutes.

JAKE   I can't believe I'm having a conversation with myself and losing the argument . . . Okay. Sit here . . . No. Stand back. Over there. In the shadow.

JULIE   Why?

JAKE   I don't know why. Because I'm nervous. I think we're playing with fire here.

JULIE   I'll take care of it, Jake. I'll treat it with respect.

JAKE   This is going to end up a famous case history. Right up there with the Elephant Man . . . Alright, here we go. *(He turns to think, then stops)* How old?

JULIE   Who?

JAKE   Molly. How old do you want her to be?

JULIE   Now. Today. All grown up. The way I've never
seen her. The way she's never seen me . . . I'm ready,
Jake.

(She goes back into the shadows)

JAKE   . . . Alright. Show time.

*(He turns away and then MOLLY comes out. She is
twenty-one and wearing the exact same brown suede
jacket that JULIE is wearing. MOLLY doesn't see JULIE
yet. She just looks at JAKE)*

MOLLY   Hi, Dad. You okay?

JAKE   Yes, honey. I'm fine.

MOLLY   So why am I here? You sure you're not sick or
anything?

JAKE   No, no. I just er . . . well, this may seem very weird
to you, Molly.

MOLLY   What is it?

JAKE   There's somebody here.

*(He looks at JULIE. MOLLY turns and sees JULIE as
well. She seems shocked at first; she takes a step back,
frightened)*

JULIE   Hello, Molly. *(MOLLY is confused)* It's alright,
Molly. Don't be afraid . . . Jake, she's having trouble
with it. It's not right this way. Help her to accept it.
Oh, Molly, I didn't want to scare you.

JAKE   Okay. I didn't think it out. Let me start over . . .

MOLLY   NO! It's alright . . . Now I understand. Now it's fine.

JULIE   Are you sure?

MOLLY   Yes. Positive . . . Hello, Mom.

JULIE   Hello, Molly . . . Would you like to sit down here with me? Would that be alright?

MOLLY   Yes. Of course. *(She goes and sits on the sofa next to JULIE)* I have a million things to ask you. It's like meeting someone you've always heard about. Like a movie star. Only it's my mom. I feel like asking you for your autograph.

JULIE   I love the way you look, Molly. We have a classy-looking daughter, don't we, Jake?

JAKE   Yes, Julie.

JULIE   Do I seem very different from the way you remembered me?

MOLLY   You're prettier than your pictures. And you look younger than I thought you'd be.

JULIE   Your father touched me up a little.

MOLLY   I didn't even realize it. We're wearing the same jacket.

JULIE   Isn't it great? Your dad prints them out like Xerox copies. *(She looks at MOLLY's hand. She wears four different rings)* These rings are beautiful. Where did you get them?

MOLLY   Well, this one was yours.

JULIE   Yes. It was my favorite.

MOLLY   This one Dad gave me for my sixteenth birthday. And this one Maggie gave me for Christmas. And this one a friend of mine gave me.

JULIE   Okay. Let's hear about the friend. This is the kind of news I came back for. Who is he?

MOLLY   Well, he's at Yale. The Drama Department. I met him at the theatre. He did a play there.

JULIE   An actor?

MOLLY   No. Set designer. Graduated with an architectural degree . . .

> *(MOLLY and JULIE continue talking but they mime what they're saying, keeping up the same joy and exuberance. JAKE turns to the audience)*

JAKE *(To the audience)*   I'm standing there listening to a conversation that never existed and never could. And yet it's so real to me, and from the looks of it, so real to them . . . Their joy, their laughter, the reborn intimacy and love they're sharing were created by me.

And I'm thinking, if I can create *this* intimacy, why can't I experience it in my own life?

MOLLY What was the best thing we ever did together? Just you and me.

JULIE Oh, gosh. So many things. The first movie I ever took you to see.

MOLLY *101 Dalmatians.*

JULIE Right. The first horse I ever put you on.

MOLLY Chiquita. A palomino with a yellow mane.

JULIE The first sleep-over date you ever had.

MOLLY Cynthia Gribble. She got sick in the night and threw up all over me.

JULIE And you came into my room and said, "Mommy. Cynthia just hurt my feelings." *(They both laugh at this)* What were *your* favorite times?

MOLLY That's easy. When we were in a hotel in Atlantic City. And you let me call room service and order my own dinner.

JULIE And I came out of the shower and found two chocolate sundaes and a pineapple cheesecake.

MOLLY And I thought you were the greatest mom in the whole world because you didn't send it back.

(They continue their conversation in mime. JAKE turns to the audience)

JAKE *(To the audience)*   Am I the only one who's ever done this? I don't think so. There's not one of you who hasn't thought, at three o'clock in the morning staring up at a ceiling, of what it would be like to talk to your father who died five or twenty years ago. Would he look the same? Would you still be his little girl? ... Or the boy you loved in college who married someone else. What would your life be if he proposed to you instead? ... You've played that scene out. We *all* do it ... My problem is I never *stop* doing it.

MOLLY *(To JULIE)*   ... I never wanted it to end. I never wanted to grow up ... I never wanted you to grow old ... Oh ... I'm sorry.

JULIE   That's alright, sweetheart.

MOLLY   No, it was terrible of me to say.

JULIE   It was terrible of me to leave. You must have been so angry.

MOLLY   No, not angry. I just never knew where you went to. It happened so fast. I kept thinking you'd come back but all I had was your picture next to my bed. And I would talk to it every night. Sometimes it would smile at me and sometimes I could hear your voice so clear, so comforting. Telling me what to do. Telling me not to worry. Telling me that you loved me ... Until one day I stopped hearing it. I would call out for you but there was no answer. I would shake the picture, "Talk to me. Talk to me," . . . but it would just stare back at me . . . and I felt so—cheated.

JULIE I'm sorry about that, Molly. I'm sorry about all the years we didn't have together.

JAKE *(To the audience)* And suddenly I felt this was going too far . . . *(To MOLLY)* It's getting late, Molly. Maggie'll be here soon.

MOLLY No, not yet. *(To JULIE)* Tell me other things, Mom. *Any*thing. Just keep talking.

JULIE I can't, hon. Maggie's coming over. We should go. We've taken enough of Dad's time.

MOLLY It's *not* Dad's time. It's *our* time. I don't want you to go.

JAKE We'll do it again, Molly. Another time.

MOLLY *What* other time? I've been waiting for this day since I'm ten years old. I don't want her to go.

JULIE It's alright, baby. Your father kept his promise to me, he'll keep it to you. I'll come back, I swear.

MOLLY NO! You said that to me in Vermont and you never came back. I don't trust you anymore. I don't trust him. I don't trust *any*one.

JAKE *(To the audience)* That sounds familiar. That word doesn't keep coming up by accident.

MOLLY *(To JULIE)*   I need those years. I need you to fill
in the eleven years I never had with you. Don't leave
me now when we have a chance to make them up.

JAKE   Molly, nobody can make up eleven years. Not like
this. This is just a game. We can't keep playing this
game forever.

MOLLY   I didn't ask to play it. You brought me here. You
brought Mom. You bring us together after eleven years
and you give us ten lousy minutes together. What is
that? Why did you do it? It's so damn cruel.

JULIE   Because I asked for it, Molly.

MOLLY   No, you didn't. *He* did. *He* brought us here. We
can't get here until he thinks of it. *(To JAKE)* So what
are you going to do? It's *your* goddamn game, *you* get
us out of it.

JULIE   Molly, don't.

MOLLY *(To JAKE)*   Why didn't you leave well enough
alone? What is it you wanted to see?

JAKE   I wanted to see you both happy.

MOLLY   By doing the impossible?

JAKE   Not so impossible. I saw you both laughing, both
together again. It made me happy to see that.

MOLLY   I think you're the one who doesn't know it's a
game. So what happens to us now? Do we go back in

some corner of your mind and wait till Mom's next birthday to hear the second installment of the Years That Never Happened?

JULIE Jake, stop this. I don't want to hear any more.

MOLLY He can't stop it. He loves it too much. He'll never let go of it. He'll sit in this house alone, afraid to get on with his life because this *is* his life. Isn't that right, Dad?

JAKE So everyone tells me.

MOLLY Then please let go of this.

JAKE I will. Eventually.

MOLLY No, not eventually. Eventually has come. Eventually is today. I don't know what it is you're trying to work out. If it's Mom's death, that wasn't your fault. My loss wasn't your fault.

JAKE You don't have to be at fault to feel guilty.

MOLLY You don't have to feel guilty to make it better . . . So I think Mom and I ought to go now, don't you?

JAKE It feels like someone's taking my toys away from me.

MOLLY Everybody gives up their toys sometime . . . Come on, Mom. Let's go.

JAKE Don't leave together.

115

MOLLY   Why not? The neighbors?

JAKE   It's too dramatic. Too final. Too wrapped up. I feel like Ethel Merman's going to come out and sing "Everything's Coming Up Roses" . . . Just leave, say good night, go back to school, say "See you next week."

MOLLY   That's still playing the game, isn't it?

JAKE   Sure. But indulge me.

MOLLY   Why not? *(She looks at her watch, grabs her books)* My God, what am I doing here so late? I've got exams tomorrow. Good night, Dad. Get some sleep. You look tired. *(She kisses his cheek)* Love you . . . Good night, Mom. It was real good seeing you. You look just great.

JULIE *(To JAKE)*   Can I kiss her goodbye? I won't make an opera out of it.

JAKE   Whatever you like. I'm not playing anymore.

(JULIE turns and looks at MOLLY, who rushes into JULIE's arms. They embrace)

JULIE   I love you, baby.

MOLLY   I love you, Mom.

(She turns and rushes off)

JULIE   Thank you for my present, Jake.

JAKE Next time you're getting a gift certificate from Bendel's. *(The doorbell rings)* That's Maggie. You'd better go.

JULIE Not yet. You still have one more thing to do for me.

JAKE Don't ask to see Bark. He died when he was twelve.

JULIE I want a proper kiss goodbye.

JAKE Oh, I don't think we should get physical, Julie. They have a nasty word for that.

JULIE *(She moves closer, puts her arms around his neck)* You don't have to do a thing. This one is my fantasy. *(They kiss, warmly and deeply. The doorbell rings again)* Goodbye, Jake.

(MAGGIE enters)

MAGGIE Hi.

JAKE Hi.

MAGGIE It's good to see you.

JAKE You look wonderful.

JULIE Don't screw this up, Jake.

(She leaves)

JAKE *(To MAGGIE)* How are you feeling?

MAGGIE Tense but relaxed . . . How about you?

JAKE I'm studiously nonchalant.

MAGGIE The apartment looks nice. Anything new here?

JAKE Just today's paper . . . How's your apartment?

MAGGIE Ugly. But it has a very nice view of better apartments.

JAKE You look very fit. Still jogging?

MAGGIE No. Treadmill. I like running in place. I don't have that same urge to get somewhere.

JAKE You can sit down, if you like. I think that's your half of the sofa there.

MAGGIE Oh, er, if you get a letter from my lawyer about a legal separation, you can forget about it.

JAKE Really? Change your mind?

MAGGIE No. He died . . . I have to get a new lawyer.

JAKE Doesn't everyone? . . . Can I get you anything? A drink? Coffee?

MAGGIE No, thanks. I'm meeting dinner for someone . . . Someone for dinner . . . Okay, so I *am* a little nervous.

JAKE   Yeah, well, this smile is painted on, too. So, what's this new job of yours I hear about?

MAGGIE   Yes. I'm working for Wang.

JAKE *(He nods)*   What's he like?

MAGGIE   Well, there really isn't a Wang. It's that computer company with the oblique commercials. Five men and a woman sitting around a table with overlapping conversations and quick cuts to their shoes or scratching their earlobes. It's a very effective ad campaign except that most people still don't know what a Wang is.

JAKE   I *thought* I knew but it couldn't be the same thing.

MAGGIE   No, I don't think so . . . Oh, Christ, Jake. I'm so glad we got the first part of this conversation over with.

JAKE   I know. I felt like we wandered into a Noel Coward tribute or something.

MAGGIE   You *are* funny, Jake.

JAKE   And what about you? Are you happy?

MAGGIE   Happy? . . . No, not really. But at least I'm not running like mad trying to find it everywhere from here to Calcutta.

JAKE *(He smiles)*   Calcutta! . . . That reminds me of that

three-way conversation we had with Sheila. That was
something, wasn't it?

MAGGIE   Who's Sheila?

JAKE *(He pauses, looks at her)*   Shit! Sorry. Just having a
minor lapse with my spatial concepts.

MAGGIE   Still can't keep them out, heh, Jake . . . God, the
irony of it.

JAKE   Of what?

MAGGIE   That I'm still attracted to the very thing about
you that drove me out of here.

JAKE   That sounds promising.

MAGGIE   I didn't make any. I still don't think a marriage
can run on an attraction.

JAKE   No, I don't think so either . . . So what brings you
here?

MAGGIE   I just wanted to see you. To talk to you.

JAKE   I sense something important is about to be said.

MAGGIE   I think the man I'm going to have dinner with
tonight is going to propose to me.

JAKE   I see. Well, that qualifies as important. Probably in
the same category as "My house is on fire" . . . How
do you feel about it?

MAGGIE   I'm scared I might say yes.

JAKE   Who isn't? . . . And what's the frightening part?

MAGGIE   That it would be over with us.

JAKE   Well, it would certainly slow us down . . . I don't
suppose I could come along and coach you? . . . No
. . . What does he do?

MAGGIE   He listens to me. He pays attention.

JAKE   You mean for a living?

MAGGIE   Jesus!

JAKE   What?

MAGGIE   I'm sitting here telling you that in twenty minutes I may be making the biggest decision of my life
and I don't feel any concern from you or any interest
in my life unless it's connected to you.

JAKE   I'm concerned. If you got sick, I would worry. If
you got married, I'd be pissed . . . Since I still care for
you, that seems pretty reasonable to me.

MAGGIE   I still care for you too, Jake. But it doesn't depend on our getting together or not.

JAKE   Am I dense because I'm not rooting for the other
guy to get the girl?

MAGGIE   No matter what we talk about, it always seems
to come out like a story conference.

JAKE   Well, if it is, I never seem to get past the editor. Christ, Maggie, if we're just going to pick up where we left off six months ago, you should have gone straight to dinner.

MAGGIE   I was hoping that things might have changed since six months ago.

JAKE   *(He shrugs)*   They have. You found a guy who listens better than I do.

MAGGIE   Don't listen to the words, Jake. Listen to the feelings. There's pain going on here. Your pain and mine. And we can't get anywhere until we get in touch with those feelings. We're like two people reaching out for each other with both hands tied behind our backs.

JAKE *(Confused)*   Why can't I understand your concept of getting in touch with pain? I don't think I just speak words. I speak feelings and emotions. I care. I love. I'm miserable. I'm angry. I'm desperate. I'm hopeful and mostly I'm confused. Am I getting close?

MAGGIE   Yes, Jake. You're getting close.

JAKE   Thank God. Tell me what I did so I can hold on to it.

MAGGIE   I think part of you is standing right there in front of me, listening and talking to me . . . But there's that other part of you. The writer. The observer who's standing up there in his office, right now, watching and observing the two of us, detached as hell, and *he's* the one who's getting in our way, Jake. He's the one who's not involved in our problem. He's a voyeur. A manipulator. And unless you can let go of him and trust yourself, Jake, trust how you feel and not what he judges to be the truth, then you'll never feel safe with me or with anyone . . . And that would be such a loss . . .

JAKE   Jesus, Maggie, you make me feel so isolated. So inhuman.

MAGGIE   No. I think you're alone. I think you put yourself there a long time ago because it feels safe to you. All that I'm asking is that you come out of your hiding place and join the rest of us. There's a lot of people out here who love you, Jake. Trust it.

JAKE   *(Hoping to explain)*   I don't observe because I choose to. I'm not alone because I prefer it. I'm not a writer because I'm good at it . . . I write to survive. It's the only thing that doesn't reject me. My characters are the only ones I know who love me unconditionally, because I give them life. Do you love me unconditionally, Maggie?

MAGGIE   I'm not that selfless. And you didn't give me life, Jake. My mother did. And I like you much better than I like her.

JAKE   Do you? Funny, you look about ten miles away from where I sit.

MAGGIE   No, Jake. I think we're so close. I swear. I think we're only an inch or two apart.

JAKE   What's wrong with that? Most couples I know
have the Grand Canyon between them and they don't
even notice.

MAGGIE   I notice. But I want more than that for us.

JAKE   I mean this in all sincerity. I wish I were as smart
as you.

MAGGIE   I wasn't this smart before I married you. You
made me think. You made me observe.

JAKE   So why doesn't your observer run off with *my*
observer and you and I can stay here?

MAGGIE   Okay. If you want me to stay, I'll stay. If you
want me to come back, I'll come back.

JAKE   *(He smiles)*   You're tricky, you really are. You
know I'd grab that in a minute. But you're also smart
enough to know that I'm smart enough to know that
wouldn't work. That I know you're right. That until
I cross those two inches, until I can understand the
concept of those two inches, we'd always be in trouble.

MAGGIE   You know something, Jake. Even though we've
just been pretty tough on each other, this is one of the
best talks we've ever had.

JAKE   Really? I hated it. I grew up seeing movies where
saying "I love you" was a happy ending.

MAGGIE   Maybe it will be. Once we both realize this isn't
a movie . . . I'm late for dinner.

JAKE   You're not really going to say yes to him tonight, are you? I mean, is this guy only a quarter of an inch away from you or what?

MAGGIE   No, I'm not going to say yes . . . I'm going to wait till I hear from you.

JAKE   Oh, you're just going to leave me walking around here all day with a tape measure? What are you hoping is going to happen?

MAGGIE   A catharsis! A bolt of lightning! A miracle!

JAKE   Jesus, now I have to be the Messiah.

MAGGIE   No, I'll just settle for Jake . . . So long, Jake.

(She goes)

JAKE *(To the audience)*   Men have climbed mountains for women and crossed burning deserts for them, and I can't get to this one because I'm two lousy inches away . . . Maybe if I put a little weight on around the midsection, I could squeeze across the finish line . . . Okay, so I need a catharsis, a bolt of lightning and a miracle . . . Where the hell do you shop for that . . . Wait! Hold it! . . . One last Mother story . . . Make that a Mother and Father story . . . I feel a connection here . . . I am ten years old, walking down the street with my friend, Sal . . . And coming in the opposite direction is my father with a woman half his age . . . A chippie, they called them then . . . He doesn't see me but Sal says to me, "Hey, Jake. There's your father" . . . And I say to protect my father or my shame, "No, it's not. He just *looks* like my father" ... What prompts me later that day to tell my mother about it is still unclear to me. I want to make things right but right for who? ... When my father comes home later that night, my mother pulls him into my bedroom, turns on the lights and screams at me, "Tell him, Jake. Tell him what you told me you saw today" ... I want to run as fast as I can or die on the spot, but my mother won't be denied. I tell my father what I saw ... And he looks me in the eye and says, "You're a liar. You saw someone else, not me" ... He makes me pay for his indiscretion ... I hate my father for betraying my mother, hate my mother for betraying me and hate myself for betraying them both ... It did, in time, pass and maybe was even forgotten in the forty years that eventually buried them both ... But I can't help feeling that three betrayals in one day could eventually make two inches to cross—a very long trip for someone who never learned to trust again ... So what would that be? A small catharsis? ... *(He looks off)* What do you think, Karen? ... Karen? ... Where are you? ... Karen, I'm calling you. *(To the audience)* She's never done this before ... Karen, it's Jake. I need you ... Come on, wear anything you want, I'll pay for it. Where are you? *(To the audience)* This is scary. Don't go away. I don't feel like being alone right now ... Edith! ... Please come out. I can't wait till our appointment on Tuesday ... I need a quick fix. A couple of laughs ... I need the jokes, the kidding around. *Love Yourself, Fuck Them,* that was funny, wasn't it? ... Molly? Julie? Not even you? ... You want to see each other again, I'll set it up. I'll order in pizzas, you can spend the whole day gabbing and gorging yourselves, whaddya say? *(To the audience)* Jesus! I've been praying to get rid of them, *begging* for them to be

gone and now that they're not here I feel empty. I feel
scared, I feel stark naked . . . Jesus, this is hard. My
goddamn heart is palpitating . . . I can hardly breathe
. . . what is this? . . . Is this going crazy? Is this going
mad? . . . Or is this the miracle? . . . I mean she already
got her catharsis, maybe this is the freaking miracle
. . . *(He looks around)* So what have we got left? A bolt
of lightning . . . *(He moves away)* Better get away from
anything metal . . . Rubber? Where's rubber? . . .

*(He looks around. We suddenly hear a VOICE, a
VOICE not clear as to gender or age)*

VOICE "Jake, are you alright?"

JAKE *(He looks up)* No! . . . I'm not alright . . . Who is
that? Karen?

VOICE *(From another speaker)* Are you alright, Jake?

JAKE I just said no, didn't I? . . . Why, do I look alright?
I'm falling to pieces here . . .

VOICE *(From another speaker)* Jake, are you alright?

JAKE *(To the audience)* What is this, *Field of Dreams?*
"Build it and they will come"? *(To VOICE)* . . . Who are
you? What do you want?

VOICE *(From another speaker)* Don't get scared, Jake.
Don't get nervous. It's me.

JAKE *(To the audience)* Oh, my God. I think it's my
mother. *(To VOICE, cautiously)* Mom? Is that you? *(To*

the audience) Gee, I hope she didn't hear me tell about the dirt turning into roaches.

VOICE *(From another speaker)* I love you . . . and I forgive you.

JAKE You forgive *me*? *(Somewhat sarcastic)* Well, that's very generous of you, Mom . . . Why can't I see you? Where are you?

VOICE *(From another speaker)* I love you . . . and I forgive you.

JAKE What have you got, your own sound system? . . . What are you doing this for, Mom? . . . If you forgive me, what is it you forgive me for? *(To the audience)* Am I really hearing her or is this my imagination? . . . No, this is coming from someplace else . . . Some deep place I've never tapped into before. Only what's the point of it? *(To VOICE)* What are you doing this for, Ma?

VOICE *(From another speaker)* Think about it, Jake. You'll figure it out.

JAKE *(To the audience)* Thank God Sheila isn't here, her hair would turn white by now . . . "Think about it, Jake. You'll figure it out" . . . My mother was never articulate before and suddenly she gives me the hiero-glyphics to work out . . . "Think about it, you'll figure it out" . . . No, as I said, I loved my mother, but I didn't trust her before and I don't trust her now. *(He starts up the steps, stops, then comes back down)* . . . Wait a minute, wait a minute, hold it . . . That's not my mother's voice.

It didn't sound like her . . . It sounded like—like me
. . . Jesus! It was *my* voice. I had it all turned around
. . . It was *me* saying to my mother, "I love you, Mom
. . . and I forgive you" . . . *(He stops, catches himself,
moves toward the audience)* I love you, Mom . . . and I
forgive you. *(He takes a second, then looks at the audience)*
I think you have to forgive those you love before you
can forgive yourself . . . And so Maggie got her bolt of
lightning. *(He starts up to his office)* So what do I do
now? Call the restaurant and say to the maître d',
"Please tell the pretty lady in the beige suit her husband
called and said, 'Just had the big three. Hurry home' "?
. . . *(He sits at his desk)* No. Nothing in life gets resolved
that fast. *(He turns and looks at the word processor, when
suddenly we hear music from downstairs. To the audience)*
Did I leave the stereo on? . . . Or are my imaginary
conversations turning into musicals now?

> *(OLDER MOLLY, EDITH, KAREN, JULIE, SHEILA and
> YOUNGER MOLLY all appear suddenly from doors,
> from the balconies on both sides, all in party dresses)*

ALL SIX WOMEN   Surprise!

JAKE *(To the audience)*   They're back! . . . Just when I
thought it was safe to go back to the typewriter . . .
Karen, don't! Edith, Molly, Julie, please! If you love
me, you'll go and never come back.

EDITH *(In baby talk again)*   But you need us, Jakey. You
called for us.

KAREN   We were getting dressed. I paid a fortune for
this.

YOUNGER MOLLY   Let us stay, Daddy. I love being twelve years old.

JULIE *(She hugs OLDER MOLLY)*   And Molly and I can be together forever, Jake.

OLDER MOLLY   Can we, Dad?

SHEILA   If you want, I'll go to Calcutta, Jake. I'll quit my job.

JAKE   No! No! NO! I don't want that.

EDITH   Then what do you want? Ask for it, Jake. Please! ASK FOR IT!

JAKE *(He shouts)*   MAGGIE! I WANT MAGGIE!

EDITH   Oh! *(She smiles)* Well, it's about time, Jake.

(The doorbell rings. They all turn and look. MAGGIE comes in, in the outfit she was just wearing)

JULIE   Let's go, ladies . . . I don't think we live here any more.

(One by one, they quickly disappear)

MAGGIE   I let myself in, Jake. Is that alright?

JAKE   No, you didn't, Maggie. I think *I* just let you in.

MAGGIE   I didn't go to that restaurant. I called him and explained . . . I'd like to stay and work out those last two inches together, Jake. Is that alright?

JAKE Yeah. That would be great. *(She starts up the stairs toward him)* NO! You stay there! I'll come down to you.

(He starts to take that first step cautiously)

MAGGIE Are you alright?

JAKE Well, a *little* nervous. It's a ten-mile drop from here to there.

(He starts again. He steps down very cautiously, as he and MAGGIE reach for each other, like God and Adam reaching out in the Sistine Chapel)
Fade to black

Since 1960, a Broadway season without a Neil Simon comedy or musical has been a rare one. His first play was *Come Blow Your Horn*, followed by the musical *Little Me*. During the 1966–67 season, *Barefoot in the Park*, *The Odd Couple*, *Sweet Charity*, and *The Star-Spangled Girl* were all running simultaneously; in the 1970–71 season, Broadway theatergoers had their choice of *Plaza Suite*, *Last of the Red Hot Lovers*, and *Promises, Promises*. Next came *The Gingerbread Lady*, *The Prisoner of Second Avenue*, *The Sunshine Boys*, *The Good Doctor*, *God's Favorite*, *California Suite*, *Chapter Two*, *They're Playing Our Song*, *I Ought to Be in Pictures*, *Fools*, a revival of *Little Me*, *Brighton Beach Memoirs*, *Biloxi Blues* (which won the Tony Award for Best Play), the female version of *The Odd Couple*, *Broadway Bound*, and *Rumors*. *Lost in Yonkers*, which won both the Tony Award for Best Play and the Pulitzer Prize for Drama in 1991, was followed by *Jake's Women*, the musical version of *The Goodbye Girl*, and *Laughter on the 23rd Floor*.

NEIL SIMON began his career in television, writing for *The Phil Silvers Show* and Sid Caesar's *Your Show of Shows*. Mr. Simon has also written for the screen: the adaptions of *Barefoot in the Park*, *The Odd Couple*, *Plaza Suite*, *Last of the Red Hot Lovers*, *The Prisoner of Second Avenue*, *The Sunshine Boys*, *California Suite*, *Chapter Two*, *I Ought to Be in Pictures*, *Brighton Beach Memoirs*, *Biloxi Blues*, and *Lost in Yonkers*. His other screenplays include *The Out-of-Towners*, *Murder by Death*, *The Goodbye Girl*, *The Cheap Detective*, *Seems Like Old Times*, *Only When I Laugh*, and *Max Dugan Returns*.

The author lives in California. He is married to Diane Lander and has three daughters, Ellen, Nancy, and Bryn.